**Foundation**

*Teacher's Guide*

# Launch into Literacy

*Jane Medwell* ◇ *Maureen Lewis*

**OXFORD**
UNIVERSITY PRESS

# OXFORD
## UNIVERSITY PRESS

Great Clarendon Street, Oxford OX2 6DP

Oxford University Press is a department of the University of Oxford.
It furthers the University's objective of excellence in research, scholarship,
and education by publishing worldwide in

Oxford New York

Athens  Auckland  Bangkok  Bogotá  Buenos Aires  Calcutta
Cape Town  Chennai  Dar es Salaam  Delhi  Florence  Hong Kong  Istanbul
Karachi  Kuala Lumpur  Madrid  Melbourne  Mexico City  Mumbai
Nairobi  Paris  São Paolo  Singapore  Taipei  Tokyo  Toronto  Warsaw

with associated companies in  Berlin  Ibadan

Oxford is a registered trade mark of Oxford University Press

British Library Cataloguing in Publication data

Data available

Photographs by: The Stock Market / Ariel Skelley (cover); Cluck Savage;
Corbis UK Ltd / Kevin Flemming

We are grateful for permission to reproduce the following copyright material in
this book: Marshmallow Treats recipe, from Kellogg Company; Libby Purves:
extract from The Hurricane Tree, illustrated by P. Lamont (Bodley Head), reproduced
by permission of Random House UK Ltd; Judith Nicholls: 'Did You Really?',
copyright © Judith Nicholls 1998, reproduced by permission of the author.

Illustrated by: Alan Marks, Rhian Nest James, Merida Woodford, Jane Bottomley

We have made every effort to trace and contact copyright holders
before publication. If notified, we will be pleased to rectify any error
or omissions where we have been unsuccessful.

The Publishers would like to thank all those teachers and children who
trialled and advised on this material, and on the accompanying pupils' book
in particular Georgina Ellinas, Heathery Knowe Primary, Glasgow,
St Lukes Primary, Beeston Leeds, Fair Oak Primary, Eastleigh,
Tamerton Vale Primary, Plymouth, Horrabridge Primary, Yelverton,
Rushmere Hall Primary, Ipswich, Jessop Primary, London

ISBN 0 19 915713 8

Printed in Great Britain by Information Press Eynsham.

# Contents

Introduction . . . . . . . . . . . . . . . . . . . . . . . . . . . . . . . . . . . . . . . . . . . . . . . 7
Range of texts . . . . . . . . . . . . . . . . . . . . . . . . . . . . . . . . . . . . . . . . . . . . 7
Language study levels . . . . . . . . . . . . . . . . . . . . . . . . . . . . . . . . . . . . . 7
Teaching strategies . . . . . . . . . . . . . . . . . . . . . . . . . . . . . . . . . . . . . . . 8
Progression and target setting . . . . . . . . . . . . . . . . . . . . . . . . . . . . . 8

Using the Foundation Book . . . . . . . . . . . . . . . . . . . . . . . . . . . . . . . . . . 9
Planning and target setting . . . . . . . . . . . . . . . . . . . . . . . . . . . . . . . . 9
Teaching the units . . . . . . . . . . . . . . . . . . . . . . . . . . . . . . . . . . . . . . . 9
Assessing the units . . . . . . . . . . . . . . . . . . . . . . . . . . . . . . . . . . . . . . 12
Links with the National Curricula and
the National Literacy Framework . . . . . . . . . . . . . . . . . . . . . . . . . . . . 13
NLS exemplar weekly plan . . . . . . . . . . . . . . . . . . . . . . . . . . . . . . . . . 14

## Writing to instruct

Unit 1 contents . . . . . . . . . . . . . . . . . . . . . 15

**LEAD LESSON** **Writing to instruct**

*Instructions* . . . . . . . . . . . . . . . . . . . . . . . 16

Comprehension . . . . . . . . . . . . . . . . . . . . 19

Events in order . . . . . . . . . . . . . . . . . . . . . 20

Sentences . . . . . . . . . . . . . . . . . . . . . . . . . 20

Capital letters and full stops . . . . . . . . . 21

Nouns – words that name . . . . . . . . . . . 22

Alphabetical order . . . . . . . . . . . . . . . . . 23

Writing directions . . . . . . . . . . . . . . . . . . 24

Words for places . . . . . . . . . . . . . . . . . . . 24

Verbs . . . . . . . . . . . . . . . . . . . . . . . . . . . . 25

Commands . . . . . . . . . . . . . . . . . . . . . . . . 26

Writing instructions . . . . . . . . . . . . . . . . . 27

Assessment record sheet . . . . . . . . . . . . . 29

PCM 1 *Events in order* . . . . . . . . . . . . . . 30

PCM 2 *Sentences* . . . . . . . . . . . . . . . . . . 31

PCM 3 *Nouns* . . . . . . . . . . . . . . . . . . . . . 32

PCM 4 *Alphabetical order* . . . . . . . . . . . 33

PCM 5 *Prepositions* . . . . . . . . . . . . . . . . 34

PCM 6 *Verbs* . . . . . . . . . . . . . . . . . . . . . . 35

PCM 7 *Commands* . . . . . . . . . . . . . . . . . 36

PCM 8 Instructions . . . . . . . . . . . . . . . . . 37

# Writing to entertain

Unit 2 contents .................... 38

LEAD LESSON **Writing to entertain**

*Story* ............... 39

Character and settings .............. 42

Months and seasons ............. 42

Adjectives – describing words ........ 43

Descriptions .............. 44

Verbs in stories ................ 45

Tenses .................. 45

Fiction and non-fiction ........... 46

Time order .................. 47

Homophones ................. 47

Characters speaking .............. 48

Writing a story ..................... 49

Assessment record sheet ............ 51

PCM 9 *Months and seasons* .......... 52

PCM 10 *Adjectives* ............... 53

PCM 11 *Descriptions* ............. 54

PCM 12 *Verbs* ................. 55

PCM 13 *Tense* ............... 56

PCM 14 *Fiction and non-fiction* ........ 57

PCM 15 *Homophones* ............ 58

PCM 16 *Direct speech* ............. 59

PCM 17 *Story plan 1* ............. 60

PCM 17 *Story plan 2* ............. 61

PCM 19 *A character web* ........... 62

# Writing to express

Unit 3 Contents ..................... 63

LEAD LESSON **Writing to express**

*Poem* .................... 64

Using words ................... 67

Verbs ...................... 68

Speech in bubbles ............... 68

Rhyming couplets ............... 69

Question poems .............. 70

Noisy words .................. 71

What nonsense! .............. 71

The same but different ............ 72

Limericks ..................... 73

Writing a funny verse ............... 73

Assessment record sheet ............ 75

PCM 20 *More silly food* .............. 76

PCM 21 *Rhymes* ................ 77

PCM 22 *Vowels and consonants* ....... 78

PCM 23 *New nursery rhymes* ......... 79

PCM 24 *Riddles* ................. 80

PCM 25 *Calendar/time words* ....... 81

PCM 26 *Homographs* ............. 82

# Writing to report

Unit 4 contents ..................... 83

LEAD LESSON **Writing to report**

Report .......................... 84

Festivals and celebrations ............ 88

Celebration cards .................... 89

Writing invitations .................. 90

Using adjectives .................... 91

Adding detail ...................... 91

Describing a game .................. 92

Using charts ....................... 93

Exclamation marks .................. 94

Commas in lists .................... 94

Writing a report ................... 95

Assessment record sheet ............. 97

PCM 27 *Celebration cards* ........... 98

PCM 28 *Days of the week* ........... 99

PCM 29 *Rebus invitations* ........... 100

PCM 30 *Describing toys* ............. 101

PCM 31 *Plurals* .................... 102

PCM 32 *Alphabetical order* .......... 103

PCM 33 *Months of the year* ......... 104

PCM 34 *Commas in lists* ............ 105

# General photocopy masters

Introduction ....................... 106

PCM 35 *2 column sheet* ............ 107

PCM 36 *3 column sheet* ............ 108

PCM 37 *Flow chart for sequence events*
.............................. 109

PCM 38 *Drafting code* ............. 110

# Assessment copymasters

PCM 39 *Play the Dictionary Game* ....111

PCM 40 *The Seal King's Daughter* ....112

PCM 41 *Comprehension* ............113

PCM 42 *Sequencing a story* .........114

PCM 43 *Fiction and non-fiction* ......115

PCM 44 *Grammar activity: sentences* ..116

PCM 45 *Punctuation: writing speech* ...117

PCM 46 *Riddles and rhyme* ..........118

PCM 47 *Planning a postcard* .........119

PCM 48 *Writing a postcard* ..........120

Assessment record sheet ............121

Glossary ..........................122

# Introduction

Oxford Literacy Web is a range of materials which enable you to meet the literacy demands of your curriculum (NC or 5–14). The materials offer full literacy coverage and are designed for current teaching methods.

All the materials have been designed with a number of principles in mind:

- that children need structured experience of a full range of text types
- that children need to learn how language works at a word, sentence and text level
- that literacy is best learned through demonstration, guided practice and experimentation
- that children benefit from direct whole-class teaching, teacher-led group work, and independent activities.

On the basis of these principles Oxford Literacy Web provides an appropriate range of texts to study all levels of text using effective teaching strategies.

## Range of texts

*Launch into Literacy* addresses the reading, writing and study of a full range of text types. Each unit is designed to take children at least 15 hours and is based around the study of a particular genre or a purpose for writing. Six main purposes are included to cover major fiction and non-fiction genres:

- Writing to entertain - the major types of fiction, including stories and plays
- Writing to express – poetry
- Writing to report – recount and report
- Writing to persuade – persuasion and argument
- Writing to explain – explanations
- Writing to instruct – instructions and directions.

In each language unit, children read, write and study a number of texts, undertake activities related to the key language points and then produce a text in the same genre.

## Language study levels

*Launch into Literacy* structures the ways children study the sentence and word level features of texts in the context of whole texts, so that children not only study words, grammar and punctuation but also how these text levels are connected.

Each language unit begins with a study text. The whole class analyse the content, structural features and language features of a particular text. The language unit then provides exercises for children to study the text, sentence and word level language features emphasized in the text analysis. Each language unit includes activities addressing:

- comprehension and other reading skills (dictionaries, etc.)
- composition (planning, drafting, revising and editing)
- text level language features and structures
- grammar
- punctuation
- word study (including vocabulary, word structure and word origins).

The knowledge and skills gained in the exercises are used to write a final text, and can be assessed at this time.

## Teaching strategies

*Launch into Literacy* is designed be used for direct whole-class teaching, group activities and independent practice.

Each unit includes:

- A lead lesson which should be taught by the teacher in one long or three short whole-class sessions. Teachers use shared reading of a demonstration text and questioning to examine the content, structural and language features of the text.
- A mid-unit whole-class teaching session in which shared reading and questioning are used to focus again on the content, structural and language features of this text type.
- Follow-up activities for teacher-led work which introduce new grammatical, punctuation or word concepts. These sessions often involve guided reading.
- Follow-up activities for independent practice.
- Photocopy masters (PCMs) for group or individual extension and support (differentiation).
- A final set of writing tasks which can be tackled independently and are particularly well suited to assessment.

This guide contains an additional unit of assessment PCMs which revisit some of the key issues at this level. There are also general photocopiable activities for key skills.

## Progression and target-setting

*Launch into Literacy* sets ambitious targets and is designed to teach children to:

- develop flexible reading skills for fiction and non-fiction
- develop the composition skills of planning, drafting and revising
- analyse texts and how they work
- study all levels of language and how they work together
- use technical words about language (meta-language).

The Foundation Book contains four units which can be used interchangeably through the year.

Each level of the programme sets clear targets for the year and for each unit.

Each level of the programme builds on the language skills, knowledge and understanding of the previous level, as well as developing children's use of linguistic terminology.

# Using the Foundation Book

## Planning and target-setting

The Foundation Book contains activities in the following areas:

- a particular text type or genre
- composition and writing skills
- reading and comprehension skills
- knowledge of text features
- grammar
- punctuation
- word study.

The content of the Foundation Book is set out for planning purposes on pages 62-63 of the Pupil's Book. Use this table to select units which fit your scheme of work and set appropriate targets for the children in the class. Where possible all the children in the class should do the same unit at the same time to allow the maximum possible flexibility in teaching.

We recommend that teachers plan for a teacher-led session to introduce new grammatical, punctuation and word concepts or reading and writing skills. Each lesson of this type has a relevant PCM which provides either extension, practice or support work about the concept. These sheets can be used to assist with differentiation.

## Teaching the units

Each unit includes whole-class teaching sessions, teacher-led groupwork activities and independent practice activities.

In each unit of the programme two double-page spreads in the Pupils' Book are designed to be used for whole-class teacher-led sessions:

- the lead lesson at the start of each unit which contains the study text
- a double-page spread with another example text around the middle of each unit.

The other pages of the unit are designed for teacher-led group work or independent practice.

These suggested levels of support are marked on the Teacher's Guide with the following icons:

Whole-class teaching

Teacher-led activities

Activities suitable for pupils to do independently

## Whole-class teaching

It is very important to start each unit with the whole-class lead lesson, which explores the key features of the opening text. The whole text focus of the lead lesson is the setting for subsequent sentence and word level work and it is important that the children understand this so that they know why they are studying the text.

Within the structure of the literacy hour the lead lesson can be done in one of two ways:

1 Use the whole literacy hour to study all aspect of the example text with the whole class. Extend the whole-class section of the hour and do the complete lead lesson as described in the lesson plan (below, 30–40 minutes). Follow up with the first PCM to follow the unit, which is an activity related to the text, and conclude with a plenary session to examine the outcomes.

or

2 Do the lead lesson in short blocks of whole class work (10–15 minutes) on three consecutive days. The three blocks address the content, structural and language features of the text. Short blocks within the lead lesson are indicated in the lesson plan below. On these days you can continue other language tasks in the remainder of the literacy hour, and discuss outcomes during a plenary session.

The whole-class lesson in the middle of each unit can be done in similar ways. We recommend using the lead lesson over two or three consecutive days and doing the whole-class lesson in the middle of the text in a single session.

When doing these whole-class lessons you might ask the children to:

- give their superficial impressions of the text, its origins and intended audience before reading it
- read the text silently to themselves before discussing it
- read out sections of the text
- read the text in unison as you point to the words
- follow the text in the Pupils' Books as you read from the demonstration text
- answer questions about text features, sentence and word level language features, and content

- look up difficult words in the dictionary and/or speculate about their meaning

As the whole-class lesson develops it is extremely useful to mark text structures, difficult words and language features onto the demonstration text. We recommend using three different coloured pens to mark:

- content
- text level language features and text structures
- sentence and word level language features.

In this way you can build up a fully annotated text which can be revisited, perhaps in a plenary session following group activity.

During these whole-class teaching sessions it is important for you to emphasize not only the language features and structures in the text, but also the effect of these features and the way they are connected to give the text its structure and form.

**Materials required for the lead lessons:**

- demonstration poster of the lead text
- Pupils' Books for the children to follow when reading and discussing the text
- three coloured pens for use on the demonstration poster

    *pen a*, for content issues (difficult words or phrases, key details)

    *pen b*, for structural and text level language features of the text

    *pen c*, for sentence and word level features of the text
- dictionaries for teacher and pupil use.

### *Teacher-led activities*

When introducing a new reading or writing skill, or a sentence or word level concept, you may wish to work with a group. In these circumstances it may be useful to ask children to:

- identify the focus of the lesson
- refer back to the example text at the beginning of the unit and identify the feature in the example text
- read the page of the Pupils' Book silently to themselves before discussing it
- identify difficult words or ideas on the page
- look up difficult words in the dictionary and/or speculate about their meaning.

Sometimes all the groups will do activities at the same time. This offers a good chance for a plenary session to check and develop knowledge and understanding. However, if different groups do an activity at different times you can offer different introductions to suit the children in each group and follow up with a single plenary session when all groups have completed the task. When doing groupwork tasks it is important to refer back to the lead text and emphasize the role of the skill or concept being studied.

### *Independent tasks*

When a concept or skill is revisited, or is already familiar, you may wish to use one of the practice activities or PCMs as an independent task. Independent tasks will not normally require teacher support, although children will need access to a thesaurus and dictionaries.

The final double-page spread of each unit in the Pupils' Book is a set of activities which ask the children to write a text of the type they studied at the start of the unit. These tasks may be completed in a number of short sessions. It is a good idea to display material produced at the end of the unit and to discuss examples, in a spirit of *constructive* criticism, in the class.

In this Teacher's Guide there are suggestions for further activities relevant to each page of the Pupils' Book. Some of these support children who need more practice whilst others extend the concepts introduced.

## Assessing the units

Each unit offers opportunities to assess examples of children's:

- composition and writing skills
- reading and comprehension skills
- knowledge of text features of a particular text type or genre
- use of grammar
- use of punctuation
- understanding and use of aspects of word study
- use and understanding of linguistic terminology.

In whole-class sessions you will be able to observe the enthusiasm and willingness to contribute of individuals and evaluate the quality of their contributions.

Group sessions offer a good setting for detailed observation of children's skills and for discussion to probe children's understanding. You will also be able to analyse the products of sessions to assess:

- what children can do both with support and alone
- what errors and misconceptions children have made
- what further teaching and experience children require.

The final spread of each unit of the Pupils' Book is a set of activities which ask the children to write a text of the type they studied at the start of the unit. During this task you can:

- observe children as they use their reading and writing skills
- collect writing products (drafts, etc.) for analysis, discussion with children, and inclusion in profiles or portfolios.

This handbook contains a recording sheet for each unit which details the skills and knowledge involved. This sheet can be used for individual pupils or, more manageably, for recording the performance of groups of children. You may wish to use the spaces in the grids to record comments about the degree to which the child has achieved the objective, or use a code. This sheet and/or examples of children's work can be used for individual conferences with children and class discussion.

The Assessment Activity PCMs offer a range of activities which address key points from throughout the Foundation Book. They can be used when the children have completed the book to assess their understanding of the issues studied and linguistic terminology. These PCMs are slightly more demanding than the other PCMs. The activities could be used to make a separate assessment of the literacy skills and knowledge of children in the class, perhaps in the half term in which they are not doing a language unit. An assessment sheet for these PCMs is included on page 121.

## Links with National Curricula and the National Literacy Strategy Framework

This guide provides aims, teaching notes, and related activities to teach reading and writing skills to 6–7 year olds. The guide provides work at text, sentence and word level listed in the National Literacy Strategy for Year 2, and it will enable children to work at these levels:

National Curriculum in England and Wales Level 2.

English Language 5–14 (National Guidelines in Scotland) Level A.

Northern Ireland Curriculum Level 2.

## NLS exemplar weekly plan (Unit 1)

| | Whole class: Shared text work | Whole class: Sentence and word work | Guided group task | Independent group task | Independent group task | Independent group task | Independent group task | Plenary |
|---|---|---|---|---|---|---|---|---|
| **Mon** | Unit 1 p 4-5 Instructions Session 1 – Content and meaning. As in teacher's notes | Revise long vowel phonemes ow. Use 'low' & 'mallow' from lead text | Group A Guided reading | Group B Long vowel phoneme ow, grow, show, sow, etc | Group B Long vowel phoneme ow, grow, show, sow, etc | Group D Make picture strip for the recipe in shared text. Add sentences | Group E Make picture strip for the recipe in shared text. Add sentences | Make class list of long vowel words. Check picture strips for correct sequence |
| **Tues** | Same lead text. Session 2 – Text features. As in teacher's notes | Short vowel phoneme ow as in cow, how, now, bow | Group B Guided reading | Group C Make picture strip for the recipe in shared text. Add sentences | Group D Short vowel phonemes | Group E Short vowel phonemes | Group F Long vowel phoneme ow – grow, show, sow, etc | Make class list of long vowel ow words. Compare with long vowel list created on Monday |
| **Weds** | Same lead text. Session 3 – Word features. As in teacher's notes | Words that signal time/order | Group C Guided reading | Group D PCM 1 Making a drink | Group E PCM 1 Making a drink | Group A Pupils' Book Page 6 Comprehension | Group B Pupils' Book Page 6 Comprehension | Check the order words pupils have used in sentences for PCM 1 |
| **Thurs** | Start shared writing of recipe (if possible cooking groups during rest of week) | Imperative tone. (+ spelling) Common cooking commands, e.g. stir, chop, fry, boil, cut, mix | Group D Guided reading | Group E Pupils' Book Page 6 Comprehension | Group A PCM 1 Making a drink | Group B PCM 1 Making a drink | Group C Pupils' Book Page 6 Comprehension | Check pupils' sentences for imperative verbs |
| **Fri** | Shared writing continued | Puntuation of sentences. Contrast with punctuation of list (not in sentences) | Group E Guided reading | Group A Make picture strip/instructions for common classroom activity | Group B Make picture strip/instructions for common classroom activity | Group E PCM 1 Making a drink | Group E Pupils' Book Page 6 Comprehension | Discuss how punctuation and layout of list and sentence vary |

# Writing to instruct

| Pupils' Book content | Whole class  | Teacher led  | Independent  | PCM  |
|---|---|---|---|---|
| **Texts** | | | | |
| instructions | 5 | | | |
| directions | 12 | | | |
| **Text features** | | | | |
| reading | 5 | 5 | | |
| diagrams | 10 | 10 | 7 | |
| aim | 5 | 5 | | |
| chronological order | 10 | | 7 | 1 |
| **Reading skills and comprehension** | | | | |
| literal and inferential comprehension questions | 4, 12 | 4, 12 | 6 | |
| extracting information from maps | 12 | 12 | | |
| **Writing skills and composition** | | | | |
| planning | 16 | 16 | | 37 |
| making rough notes | 16 | 16 | | |
| drafting | 17 | 17 | | |
| listing | | | 6 | 8, 38 |
| labelling | 10, 13 | 10 | 7 | |
| **Grammar** | | | | |
| nouns | 10 | 10 | | |
| prepositions | 13 | 13 | | 5 |
| sentences | 8 | 8 | | 1, 2 |
| verbs | 14 | 14 | | 6 |
| commands | 15 | 15 | | 7 |
| capital letters | | | 9 | |
| **Punctuation** | | | | |
| question marks | | | 9 | |
| exclamation marks | | | 9 | |
| full stops | | | 9 | |
| **Words** | | | | |
| labels | 10, 13 | 10, 13 | | |
| technical vocab | 1–2 | 1–2 | | |
| alphabetical order | 11 | 11 | | |
| dictionary use | 11 | 11 | | 4, 39 |

**LEAD LESSON**

# Writing to instruct

## Aims of the lead lesson

- to introduce close analysis of a text
- to explore the structure of a procedural (instruction) text
- to consider the language features of a procedural (instruction) text
- to explore the layout and punctuation conventions of the text

**SESSION 1** | *Introducing the text*

### Content and meaning

*pen a*

- Point out the demonstration poster. This is a large version of the text on page 5 of the Pupils' Book. Explain that you are going to read and look closely at a piece of writing that tells the reader how to do something (instructs). Ask questions about where the text comes from and how they know. Have they seen recipes like this before? Why do manufacturers put recipes on food packets?
- Read the demonstration text aloud, pointing at the text you are reading.
- Reread the demonstration text with the children following the text in their books. Check the children's understanding of the content by asking questions such as:

  What do the instructions tell you how to make?
  Who would read this sort of text?
- Annotate any difficult words or phrases and look them up in the dictionary. (Likely words are 'blended', 'remove' and 'greased'.)
- If possible, arrange for other recipes to be available, or make a class collection from a range of sources, e.g. recipe books, magazines, cookery cards, food packets.

# OXFORD LITERACY WEB

Launch into Literacy, Foundation Book, Unit 1

# Writing to instruct
## Try this great summer recipe

aim ——— How to make Marshmallow Treats

precise information

| 25 g | butter or margarine |
| 40 g | marshmallows |
| 50 g | *Kellogg's Rice Krispies* |

a list
It has no full stops.

- Melt the butter or margarine in a saucepan.

nouns

- Add the marshmallows and stir over a low heat until the marshmallows have melted and the mixture is well blended.

events in chronological order

- Remove from the heat.

- Add the *Kellogg's Rice Krispies* and stir until well coated.

difficult words

- Press the mixture into a greased 18 cm square tin.

commands (tell us what to do)

- When cool cut into squares and then triangles.

CHILDREN: Whilst it can be great fun making Marshmallow Treats, a hot cooker can be dangerous! ALWAYS ASK AN ADULT TO HELP YOU IN THE KITCHEN.

**Makes 18**

safety warning ———

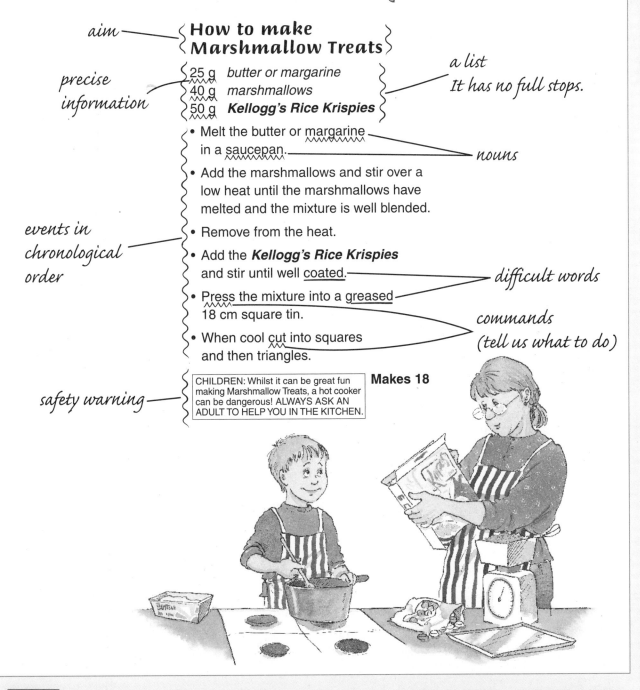

**Key**

*pen a*  Content or words to look up    *pen b*  Text features    *pen c*  Sentence and word features

*pen b*~~~~~

### Text level features

- If starting a whole-class session at this point reread the text with the class in an appropriate way. Either read it to the class or select children to read paragraphs.

- Read out (or ask children to read) the heading 'How to…'. Ask the children what the purpose of this heading is. Introduce the word 'aim' and/or 'goal' and annotate the text with the word(s).

- Read out the list of ingredients and annotate the text. Why is the list put before what you have to do? (If left to the end you might start following instructions and then realize you have not got everything you need.)

- Read out the instructions. Why are the steps are in this order? Would it matter if you did them in another order? Some instructions are numbered. Have they seen the use of roman numerals or letters to number the steps in a recipe or set of instructions?

- Recap that the whole text is in three written parts: goal, materials/equipment, and steps to be taken.

### Sentence and word level features

- If starting a third whole class session at this point reread the text with the class in an appropriate way. Select children to read paragraphs or ask the children to read silently.

- Point out that some parts of the recipe are written in a list and some as sentences. What is the difference? Why do we need sentences in some places and only a list in others?

- Which words name things? Point out nouns in the ingredients list.

- Ask children to identify the verb in the first sentence of each instruction. These verbs are all imperative verbs (they tell you what to do). Annotate the text with as much of this information as you think is appropriate for your class.

- Ask for suggestions for words they could add if they wanted to make the order clear. Add to text e.g. 'first', 'then', 'after that', 'finally' etc.

- Recap the structure and language features of procedures.

- Look at some other recipes to see if they have the same features.

## Related activities

■ Ask the children to find other examples of procedural texts and start a class collection/display.

PCM 1
TG page 30

■ Use PCM 1 (Events in order) to get children to consider the structure/language features of these texts.

PB page 6

# Comprehension

Text level

## Aims

■ to answer literal and inferential questions

■ to understand and recognize the difference between materials and equipment

## Teaching notes

The comprehension activity should build upon the lead lesson(s) and should take children no more than 20 minutes without your help.

---

### ANSWERS

1 **a** butter or margarine

**b** a saucepan

**c** a square tin

**d** stir the mixture and use a low heat

**e** 18

**f** because it could be dangerous using a pan on the top of the oven

2 **a** mixed

**b** covered

3 cooker
saucepan
wooden spoon, or something to stir the mixture
square tin
knife

---

## Related activities

■ Give the children further recipes. Ask them to make lists of materials or equipment.

■ Ideally, a group of children could make a simple recipe with the help of a classroom assistant or parent, then write the recipe and instructions for another group to try.

# Events in order

## Aims

- to arrange events in order
- to write lists
- to add labels to diagrams

## Teaching notes

Simple labels for diagrams are often nouns. Check the children understand the convention for linking labels to a diagram by drawing a line.

## Related activities

- Give the pupils simple diagrams with labels removed so they can label them.
- Develop the idea of labels by identifying that labels are usually nouns.

### ANSWERS

1 Spread margarine on two slices of bread. Grate 50 gm of cheddar cheese. sprinkle the grated cheese on one slice of bread and put the other slice of bread on top. Cut the sandwich in half.

2 How to make a cheese sandwich

3 Ingredients – cheese, bread, margarine. Equipment – knife, cheese grater

4 Check the three labels are in the right place and are spelt correctly.

# Sentences

Sentence level

## Aims

- to understand what constitutes a sentence
- to create sentences

## Teaching notes

It is important that children have a secure understanding that sentences include words in a certain order, make sense and are punctuated. In the first activity on this page it may help some children to run a finger along the sentence to see the words 'emerge'.

## ANSWERS

1
  **a** Put the tea-bag into the cup.

  **b** Pour on some hot water.

  **c** Add milk to your tea.

2
  **a** Pour some water into the kettle.

  **b** Switch the kettle on.
    (or Switch on the kettle.)

  **c** When the water boils, turn the kettle off.
    (or Turn the kettle off when the water boils.)

3
  **a** sentence

  **b** sentence

  **c** not a sentence

  **d** sentence

4 Check that sentences make sense, start with a capital letter, and end with a full stop.

## Related activities

■ Activities which draw children's attention to sentences and punctuation in written text, such as reading aloud with exaggerated intonation, are useful.

**PCM 2**
TG page 31

■ PCM 2 (Sentences) offers further practice in creating sentences.

PB page 9

# Capital letters and full stops

## Aim

Sentence level

■ to use capital letters and full stops to punctuate sentences

## Teaching notes

Sentence punctuation is a set of written conventions which help the reader to make sense of written language. Spoken language is actually clause-driven, so it is best to avoid telling children that full stops are 'where you take a breath'.

<br />

**ANSWERS**

1 D, T, K, R, I

2 **a** We are having sausages for tea.

**b** The boy ate greedily.

**c** Sally loves jam tarts.

3 **How to make tea**

First you need to pour water in the kettle. Then boil the water. Put tea-bags into the tea-pot. Pour boiling water on the tea. Pour the tea into cups or mugs. Add milk and sugar if you like.

## Related activities

■ Give pupils sequencing practice by jumbling up the lines of text in sets of instructions. When pupils rearrange the sentences their attention will be drawn to the full stops and capital letters.

■ Ask the children to write simple instructions, such as how to: clean your teeth, set up a computer for writing, etc.

*PB page 10*

# Nouns – words that name

## Aim

■ to introduce nouns

## Teaching notes

This activity deals with common nouns. Proper nouns are introduced later in the book.

**ANSWERS**

1 boy
sandwich
bread
cheese
knife
mother (*or* mum)

2 **a** mug

**b** tea-bag

**c** teapot

3 **a** The cat is sleeping.

**b** The policeman felt happy.

**c** What a huge ice-cream!

**d** The mouse ate the cheese.

4 **a** chocolate

**b** cat

**c** biscuit

**d** car

## Related activities

- Write nouns on yellow stickies or cards and label items in the classroom environment such as desk, book, chair, teacher, etc.

- PCM 3 (Nouns) offers more practice at using and identifying nouns.

PB page 11

# Alphabetical order

Word level

## Aims

- to differentiate between upper and lower-case letters
- to use alphabetical order (of the first letter only)

---

**ANSWERS**

1. **a** c, d
   **b** I, J
   **c** t, v
2. **a** g, h
   **b** V, W
   **c** e, f
3. **a** coke, lemonade, water
   **b** coffee, soup, tea
   **c** apple, banana, fig
4. First half – cup, bowl, glass, grater
   Second half – pot, spoon, whisk
5. Check that each letter of the alphabet is covered, in the right order, and that the words are spelt correctly.

---

## Related activities

- Alphabetical order games are useful for whole class or group sessions. Start with 'I packed my grandmother's trunk and I put in an…'. In turn, each child repeats the starting phrase and items listed so far and adds an item beginning with the next letter of the alphabet.

- PCM 4 (Alphabetical order) offers further practice at using alphabetical order.

# Writing directions

Text level

## Aims

- to interpret information given in a map
- to follow directions

## Teaching notes

This activity asks children to use quite sophisticated reading strategies to understand a sketch map. Many of them will need to follow the arrows on the map very carefully. Read the written directions, then go through Dervla's walk step by step.

**ANSWERS**

1   **a** station
  **b** traffic lights
  **c** park
  **d** pond
  **e** school

2   church
3   **a** on your right
  **b** on your right
  **c** on your left

## Related activities

- Children can programme either Logo or a programmable robot such as Roamer to follow certain routes, then write instructions for following the instructions they have used.
- Children can write instructions for leaving the class in the event of a fire. Emphasize walking safely and slowly.

# Words for places

## Aim

- to introduce prepositions

## Teaching notes

Prepositions describe the relationship between nouns and pronouns. It is not vital that children use the term preposition at this age, but they do need a good range of 'place' words – on, under, between, etc.

### ANSWERS

1. **a** over
   **b** down
   **c** out
   **d** on
3. Check that answers make sense and are given in complete sentences.
4. Check that labels are spelt correctly.

## Related activities

- Read *Rosie's Walk* by Pat Hutchins and get groups of children to write, illustrate and make similar books about another character's walk – Fred's walk, etc. Encourage children to use the most interesting prepositions they can.

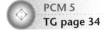

**PCM 5**
**TG page 34**

- PCM 5 (Prepositions) offers more practice at using and identifying prepositions.

**PB page 14**

# Verbs

**Sentence level**

## Aims

- to introduce verbs
- to recognize the importance of verbs in sentences

## Teaching notes

Although this page deals only with verbs of action, avoid over-simplified definitions such as 'verbs are doing words'. The verb 'to be' is studied later in the book.

**ANSWERS**

1. **a** reading
   **b** playing
   **c** swimming
   **d** eating

2. **a** runs (ran)
   **b** rolls (rolled)
   **c** bumps (bumped)

   Alternative verbs which make sense are acceptable in either the present or past tense, as long as this is used consistently.

3. **a** walks
   **b** crawls
   **c** jogs
   **d** skates

## Related activities

- Use a PE session to get children to perform the verbs you say (run, tiptoe, crawl, twirl, swoosh, etc.), changing their movement when you say a new verb.

- Alternatively, tell a simple story including some verbs – every time you say a verb the children must do it or be out of the game.

  e.g. In the morning I <u>jump</u> out of bed. Then I <u>walk</u> to the kitchen for breakfast. I <u>sit</u> down at the table. After breakfast I <u>stretch</u> myself and <u>tiptoe</u> out of the house, etc.

PCM 6
TG page 35

- PCM 6 (Verbs) offers further practice at using and identifying verbs.

PB page 15

# Commands

Text level

## Aims

- to introduce imperative sentences
- to recognize commands as a type of sentence

## Teaching notes

Commands are imperative sentences. The other three sentence types (statement, question and exclamation) are studied in this book and also in Book 1. Imperative sentences (commands) are characterized by the use of imperative verbs.

## Related activities

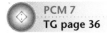
PCM 7
TG page 36

- Ask the children to make signs for use in the classroom using short imperative sentences, e.g. Sit on the mat. Put your books away.
- PCM 7 (Commands) is a further activity about commands.

### ANSWERS

| | |
|---|---|
| **1** **a** not command | **2** **a** Eat breakfast quickly. |
| **b** command | **b** Pick up the mess. |
| **c** command | **c** Jump off the wall. |
| **d** not command | |
| **e** command | **3** **a** No dogs. |
| **f** not command | **b** Throw your litter in the bin |

PB pages 16–17

# Writing instructions

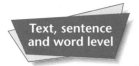
Text, sentence and word level

## Aims

- to write instructions using appropriate text and structural features (aim, technical words, chronological order)
- to use imperative sentences
- to plan using rough notes and a timeline
- to edit instructions
- to set out instructions appropriately

PCM 8
TG page 37

## Teaching notes

This activity draws together the skills used in Unit 1 so that the children can use them to write instructions about a topic of their choice. These activities can be done in one long session or as a number of shorter sessions. Doing the activities as a number of shorter sessions offers you the chance to use both products (drafts, notes, etc.) and observation for assessment purposes.

If you wish to do a teacher introduction we suggest that you take the opportunity to do a shared rereading of the instructions earlier in the unit and remind the class about the main structural features and language of instructions: statement of aim, chronological order, detail, chronological connectives and imperative sentences.

## ASSESSMENT POINTS

As you observe the children working you may wish to note whether, and to what extent, they can do the following:

### plan

- select a game
- brainstorm ideas
- discuss or answer the planning questions
- select an appropriate heading

### First draft

- write a first draft under the headings given, so that events are arranged chronologically
- use imperative sentences effectively
- use chronological connectives

### Revise

- read text through to another child
- comment on the content and/or structure of the passage with questions as guidance

### Edit

- look for any spelling, grammar and punctuation issues

**TEACHER'S OBSERVATIONS**
The brainstorm is limited but captures the main points of the game.

**TEACHER'S OBSERVATIONS**
There are some excellent features of instruction writing included in this initial draft: the use and underlining of headings and the numbering of steps. The sentences, which are generally imperative, make sense and are well punctuated. The writer has difficulty in using the impersonal type of writing usually found in instructions and wavers between personal participants (we – first person) and the more general you (second person). The spelling is generally accurate and the child has located and corrected the main error.

cards        shout out
**SNAP**
turns                  same cards

How to play snap

You need

A pack of
~~Some~~ cards

Two or three people

A table

1 One person ~~give~~ gives out the cards so that we all have the same.

2 The first person puts down a card.

3 Then the next peson puts down a card and we all take turns.

4 When you put down the same type of card as ~~the person~~ another person before you have to shout snap and you get all the card in the pile.

5 The one who gets the cards wins.

# UNIT 1 Writing to instruct

Name _____  Group _____  Date _____

| ASSESSMENT POINT<br>*Can the child:* | PB page or PCM | Comments |
|---|---|---|
| **Text level** | | |
| read and understand instructions | 4–6, 12 | |
| write *lists* set out vertically without punctuation | 6–7 | |
| plan instructions using a *brainstorming web* and *headings* | 16–17 | |
| sequence events in *chronological order* | 7, 16–17 | |
| discuss and revise instructions | 17 | |
| extract information from a sketch map and use a key | 12 | |
| draw and label a sketch map | 12 | |
| *label a diagram* | 7 | |
| produce a final draft with appropriate *punctuation* and grammar | 17 | |
| answer literal and interferential comprehension questions | 4, 6 | |
| recognize the structural features of instructions (*aim, list of equipment, sequential steps, diagrams*) | 5 | |
| **Sentence level** | | |
| recognize the importance of *word order* and *sense* in *sentences* and use these features to order them | 8 | |
| use capital letters and full stops appropriately in sentences | 9 | |
| recognize, use *verbs* in sentences | 14 | |
| recognize and use *nouns* in sentences | 10 | |
| recognize and use *prepositions* in sentences | 13 | |
| recognize and write sentences which are *commands* | 15<br>PCM7 | |
| **Word level** | | |
| use *alphabetical order* to sequence writing | 11 | |
| look up word definitions in a dictionary | 11<br>PCM 39 | |

Unit 1

# Events in order

Name _____    Date _____

The pictures below show you how to make a drink.

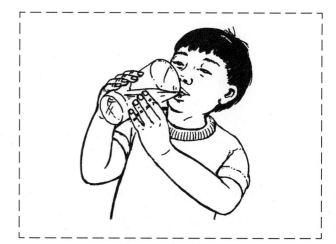

**1** Cut out the pictures and arrange them into the correct order. Number them 1–4.

**2** Write a sentence under each picture telling people what to do. Here is the beginning of the first sentence.

1. Get a glass and ....

**3** Write a title for your instructions above the pictures.

**4** Now draw four pictures and write four sentences which tell someone how to go to assembly.

# Sentences

Name _____     Date _____

Some of these sentences are not complete. Make them into complete sentences.

**Crossing the road**

1 Use a pedestrian crossing or cross with the lollipop person.

2 If you cannot do this look for a safe place to cross the road.

3 A safe place is one where you can see the

_____ .

4 Try not to cross between parked _____ .

5 _____ up and down the road to see if _____

_____ .

6 Listen for the sound of _____ .

7 When you are sure the road is clear, walk _____ .

8 Carry on looking and listening as you cross.

# Nouns

Name _____ Date _____

This is a picture from *But Where is the Green Parrot?*

**In the toy chest**

kite

1 List all the toys you can see. Start on the bottom shelf.

Use a picture dictionary if you are not sure how to spell a word.

2 Compare your list with a partner. Who has the longest list?

3 You have made a list of nouns. Write a sentence about three of the words in your list.

a _____

b _____

c _____

# *Alphabetical order*

Name _____ Date _____

| Aa | Bb | C | d | |
|----|----|----|----|----|
| f | | | I | |
| k | | M  mango | | |
| P | | r | | T |
| U | | | x | |
| z | | | | |

**1** Fill in the missing big and small letters in the alphabet square.

**2** Sort these fruit and vegetables into the correct box using the first letter of their name.

**3** Put some more fruits and vegetables into the alphabetical boxes.

# Prepositions

Name _____ Date _____

| in | on | up | down | under | behind | through |

**1** Put in the missing word from the sentences. They are all prepositions.

   **a** Claire sails _____ in the air.

   **b** Paul is walking _____ the gate.

   **c** John's feet are buried _____ lots of sand.

   **d** Ben and Betty are _____ the seesaw.

   **e** Sam climbs _____ the ladder as Josie goes _____ the slide.

   **f** Rashida peeps from _____ the tree.

**2** Now label each child with their name.

**3** One child has not got a label. Decide on a name for her.

**4** Write a sentence about the girl you have just named. Use a preposition in the sentence.

# *Verbs*

Name _____    Date _____

**1** At the Olympic games people take part in lots of different activities. Write a sentence saying what the people are doing in each of the pictures.

a _____

b _____

c _____

d _____

e _____

**2** Now underline the verb in each sentence.

**3** Write three sentences about your school sports day saying what people do during the events.

a _____

b _____

c _____

**4** Underline the verb in each of your sentences.

# Commands

Name _____    Date _____

Teachers have to give lots of commands to the class so the children know what to do.

**1** Write down four commands your teacher uses often.

**a** _____

**b** _____

**c** _____

**d** _____

Children shout commands at each other when they are playing.

**2** Write down three commands you might use when you are playing.

**a** _____

**b** _____

**c** _____

# *Instructions*

Name ................................................................................................ Date ........................................

### Drafting sheet

**Title** ................................................................................................

**The aim of the game** ............................................................................

................................................................................................................

**Equipment needed**

....................................................................  ....................................................................

....................................................................  ....................................................................

....................................................................  ....................................................................

....................................................................  ....................................................................

**What to do**

1 ................................................................................................................

................................................................................................................

2 ................................................................................................................

................................................................................................................

3 ................................................................................................................

................................................................................................................

Use these words to help your reader:
first, then, next, afterwards, finally

# Writing to entertain

| Pupils' Book content | Whole class  | Teacher led  | Independent  | PCM  |
|---|---|---|---|---|
| **Texts** | | | | |
| stories | 18–19 | 18–19 | | 9 |
| **Text features** | | | | |
| narrative opening | 18–19 | 18–19 | | 9 |
| character | 18–19 | 18–19 | | |
| setting | 18–19 | 18–19 | 20 | |
| chronological order | 18–19, 28 | 18–19, 28 | | |
| fiction/non-fiction | 26–27 | 26–27 | | 9 |
| illustrations | 18–19, 26 | 18–19, 26 | | |
| diagrams | 27 | 27 | | |
| **Reading skills** | | | | |
| literal and inferential comprehension | 26–27 | 26–27 | 20–21 | 9 |
| **Writing skills** | | | | |
| writing sentences | 22 | 22 | | |
| similes | | | 23 | |
| planning a story | | | 31 | 17, 18–19, 37 |
| drafting a story | | | 31 | 38 |
| revising a story | | | 31 | 38 |
| descriptions | | | | 11 |
| **Grammar** | | | | |
| sentences | 28 | 28 | | |
| adjectives | 22 | 22 | | 10 |
| verbs | 24 | 24 | | 12 |
| tense | 25 | 25 | | 13 |
| **Punctuation** | | | | |
| speech marks | 29 | 29 | 16 | |
| **Words** | | | | |
| months | | | 21 | 9 |
| seasons | | | 21 | 9 |
| homophones | 28 | 28 | | 15 |

PB pages 18–19

# Writing to entertain

## Aims of the lead lesson

- to identify the author and title of the story
- to examine the generic features of story openings: setting, characters and beginnings of plot (the 'who, where, when and what' of the story) and consider why an author introduces these elements.
- to identify the use and functions of adjectives and verbs in stories
- to identify written direct speech and speech marks
- to consider how the author uses language creatively and effectively

PB page 18–19

| SESSION 1 | Introducing the text |

*pen a*

### Content and meaning

- Explain that you are going to look at the opening of a short picture-book story.
- Draw the children's attention to the demonstration poster and explain that this is a large version of the text on the opening pages of Unit 2 (pages 18–19) in the Pupils' Book.
- Give the book's title and the author's name. Annotate this information on the poster. Ask children to locate this information on their own version of the text.
- If possible, show the children the actual book. Discuss the covers using the appropriate vocabulary – title, author, illustration, blurb, ISBN, etc.
- Ask what they think the story is going to be about, based on the title. Who might be in it? Where might it be set? The children should be encouraged to say why they make the predictions they do.
- Read the text, pointing to the words on the poster. Reread it with the children following in their copy. Check the children's understanding by questioning, asking children to retell, etc.
- Ask if any words are not clear. Underline any unknown words and demonstrate how to look them up in a dictionary.

# OXFORD LITERACY WEB
Launch into Literacy, Foundation Book, Unit 2

Unit 2

# Writing to entertain

## The Hurricane Tree
by L. Purves

author

title

traditional opening

Does this opening sentence catch your interest?

main character (who?)

setting (where?)

Once upon a time there was a boy called William, who lived in an old house underneath a tall tree.

In the spring, the tree was like a big pale green umbrella, higher than the rooftop, and if William looked into the branches, he could see birds building their nests.

time passing

In the summer, he had his lunch under the tree, then leaned on its smooth warm trunk and fed the crumbs to the squirrels.

In the autumn, the tree dropped sticky prickly beech nuts into William's sandpit, and threw down heaps of dry golden leaves. He made beds out of them and mountains and kicked them into snowstorms.

adjectives to add detail

snow/storm

verbs in the past tense

And in the winter, when the real snow came, his mummy sometimes took him to the kitchen window at bedtime, to see the big yellow moon at the top of the tree. "It looks like a balloon tangled up in the branches," said William. "One day, when I'm big, I'm going to climb right up that tree and sit next to the bird's nest and look at the stars."

clue to when

simile

clue to what will happen (what?)

speech marks

| Key | | | | | |
|---|---|---|---|---|---|
| **pen a** | Content or words to look up | **pen b** | Text features | **pen c** | Sentence and word features |

| SESSION 2 | *Analysing the lead text* |

*pen b* ∿∿∿∿

### Text level features of the poem

- If starting a whole-class session at this point reread the text with the class. Either read it to the class or select children to read verses.

- Stories often try to get the reader 'hooked' straight away. What does the first sentence tell us? Underline the opening sentence. Did it make you want to know more? How? Why?

- The beginning of stories usually introduces some of the main characters – the 'who' of a story. Who do they think is going to feature in this story?

- The beginnings of stories often tell us where the story is going to take place – the setting. Ask the children where they think the main part of the story might take place.

- The beginnings of stories might suggest when the story takes place – the time of day and/or, perhaps, the era. Does this story take place a long time ago or nowadays? Is there enough evidence to tell? Underline the clues.

- The beginnings of stories often give us some ideas as to what might be going to happen – the plot. Underline the clues.

| SESSION 3 | *Analysing the lead text* |

*pen c* ∿∿∿∿∿∿

### Sentence and word level

- If starting a third whole-class session at this point reread the story with the class. Either read it together or select children to read parts of the passage.

- Underline the opening sentence which begins with 'Once upon a time…' and ask about its significance. It is a traditional opening, found in many stories.

- Underline the repeated phrase 'in the …' (spring, summer, etc.). Emphasize that this signals the passing of time.

- Find and underline adjectives. Discuss their role in the sentence.

- Find and underline similes. Discuss their role in the extract. Discuss the sentence construction of a simile.

- Find and underline verbs. Discuss their tense. When is the story happening?

- Look at the passages of direct speech. Who is talking? How do the children know this?

- Finally reread the whole extract for enjoyment and understanding.

## Related activities

■ Provide a selection of story openings and ask children to compare the beginnings. What sentences catch their interest?

■ Ask the children to make a collection of the characters from stories.

■ Make a class chart of the characters and settings of favourite stories.

PB page 20

# Character and settings

## Aim

Text level

■ to answer literal and inferential questions

## Teaching notes

Children should be able to complete this in twenty minutes without help.

**ANSWERS**

**2** **a** wrote the story
**b** drew the pictures
**c** a boy called William
**d** caught in
**e** birds, squirrels
**f** an old house underneath a tall tree
**g** young – plays in sandpit, not yet big enough to climb a tree

## Related activity

■ Identify a beech tree in a reference book. Use with the opening passage to draw an illustration for the story.

PB page 21

# Months and seasons

## Aim

Sentence level

■ to establish knowledge of the months and seasons, and their order

## Teaching notes

This activity may require access to a calendar, diary or year planner. Although this activity can be done independently you may want to use a whole-class session to introduce the range of documents which use month order (diaries, calendars, etc.) or to do a shared reading of the rhyme.

Tell the children that the months of the year start with a capital letter.

### ANSWERS

**1 a** March, April, May
**b** June, July, August
**c** September, October, November
**d** December, January, February

**3 a** thirty
**b** thirty-one
**c** thirty

**4** February

## Related activities

- Look for examples of dates in newspapers and magazines and make a poster of clippings. Point out that all the months start with a capital letter.

- Make a class calendar of school events which happen in certain months, including school holidays and children's birthdays.

- Make a display of publications which use month order – calendars, diaries, almanacs, etc.

- PCM 9 (Months and seasons) offers further practice with months and seasons.

PCM 9
TG page 52

PB page 22

# Adjectives – describing words

Sentence level

## Aim

- to introduce adjectives

## Teaching notes

This activity is confined to adjectives of quality. Adjectives of quantity and number are studied in Book 2.

## Related activities

- Choose and list adjectives to describe everyday classroom nouns, e.g. wooden chair, hard floor, etc.

- PCM 10 (Adjectives) offers further practice at identifying and using adjectives.

**PCM 10**
**TG page 53**

**PB page 23**

# Descriptions

**Sentence level**

## Aim

- to identify and use similes

## Teaching notes

Similes, which create an image by comparing one thing with another, are a powerful type of description. Similes also make descriptions more interesting. It is not vital for children to know the term at this age, and it will be reintroduced in Book 1.

## Related activities

- Distribute pictures of everyday objects and ask the children to write a simile to describe them.

- PCM 11 (Descriptions) offers further activities involving adjectives.

**PCM 11**
**TG page 54**

PB page 24

# Verbs in stories

Sentence level

## Aims

- to recognize verbs and understand their role in sentences
- to use verbs and noun phrases to create sentences

## Teaching notes

Although this page deals only with verbs of action (as in Unit 1), avoid over-simplified definitions such as 'verbs are doing words'.

---

**ANSWERS**

| 1 | The sun shines. | 2 | open |
| | The rain falls. | | sing |
| | The grass grows. | | change |
| | | | fly |
| | | | go |

---

## Related activity

PCM 12
TG page 55

- PCM 12 (Verbs) offers further practice at identifying and using verbs.

---

PB page 25

# Tenses

Sentence level

## Aims

- to introduce the idea of past and present
- to use past and present tense verbs

# Teaching notes

Children have good intrinsic knowledge of tense and may use it well in speech. However, understanding the terms 'past', 'present' and 'tense' allows you to discuss their work and check for agreement and consistent use of tense.

ANSWERS

1 a and c

2 a shivered
  b ran
  c soaked

3 walk/walked
  think/thought
  hop/hopped
  blow/blew

## Related activities

**PCM 13**
**TG page 56**

- PCM 13 (Tense) offers further practice at using verb tense.
- Select 'action' pictures for children to describe using sentences beginning with either 'Today' or 'Yesterday'.

PB pages 26–27

# Fiction and non-fiction

## Aim

Text level

- to distinguish between fiction and non-fiction texts

## Teaching notes

It can be surprisingly difficult for children to distinguish between fiction and non-fiction. Non-fiction is usually characterized by certain types of illustrations (diagrams, cross-sections, etc.), page layouts (use of columns, charts, flow diagrams, etc.) and factual content. However, some non-fiction uses pictures and cartoons and some stories include factual events.

ANSWERS

2 a The Wind and the Sun
  b tells us about different wind strengths
  c breeze, hurricane, gale, storm

3 a diagrams
  b add details

## Related activities

- Provide a range of books about a topic (e.g. hedgehogs, farms, shops, schools) and ask pupils to sort them into fiction and non-fiction. The most able pupils might be able to draw up some rules for sorting.

**PCM 14**
**TG page 57**

- PCM 14 (Fiction and non-fiction) is a further activity to help children learn to distinguish between the two types of writing.

PB page 28

# Time order

Text level

## Aim

- to use chronological order

## Teaching notes

Most stories have broadly chronological sequence. This activity asks children to order a chronological sequence and reinforces the importance of chronological order in a story. It is a good idea to introduce or re-introduce the idea of chronological order.

### ANSWERS

1 c, a, d, b

2 All sentences should make sense and use capital letters and full stops. The best sentences will include time words such as 'just then', 'later', etc.

PB page 28

# Homophones

Word level

## Aim

- to use homophones and make choices based on meaning

## Teaching notes

Homophones have the same sound but different forms and different meanings (been/bean, and homographs have the same form and sound, but a different meaning ('calf' and 'calf').

### ANSWERS

1 bean: a vegetable
been: having gone
blew: a movement of air
blue: a colour
sun: hot in the sky
son: a male child

2 Sentences will either use the word in such a way as to show that the meaning is understood or define the word.

## Related activity

PCM 15
TG page 58

■ PCM 15 (Homophones) contains a reading passage using homophones and an activity which asks children to select the correct words.

PB page 29

# Characters speaking

Text and word level

## Aims

■ to introduce and use direct speech

■ to show how speech marks are used

■ to put both speech and puntuation into speech marks

## Teaching notes

This page asks children to put exactly what is said into speech marks and speech bubbles. A key point is that the punctuation which concludes a spoken sentences goes inside the speech marks, rather than outside.

---

### ANSWERS

**1** (In Manny's speech bubble) I am too hot.
(In Sanjay's speech bubble) I love the snow.
(In Jane's speech bubble) I like the autumn leaves.

**2** **a** (In the wind's speech bubble) I am stronger than you.

**b** (In the sun's speech bubble) Let us have a test to find out who is strongest.

**c** (In the man's speech bubble) Brrr, it is so cold in this wind.

**3** **a** The sun said, "Let us have a test to find out who is strongest."

**b** "I am stronger than you," said the wind.

**c** The man said, "Brrr, it is so cold in this wind."

---

PCM 16
TG page 59

## Related activity

■ PCM 16 (Direct speech) offers further practice at putting direct speech into speech marks.

# Writing a story

Text level

## Aims

- to write a story using appropriate text and structural features (setting, characters, chronological order of events)
- to use adjectives effectively in descriptions
- to plan using a chart and brainstorm web
- to edit a story
- to set out a story

PCMs 17, 18, 19
TG pages 60–62

## Teaching notes

This activity draws together the skills used in Unit 2 so that the children can use them to write a story. The activity can be done in one long session or as a number of shorter sessions. Doing the activity as a number of shorter sessions offers you the chance to use both products (drafts, notes, etc.) and observation for assessment purposes. A character web (PCM 19) and story planning sheets (PCMs 17 and 18) are provided for use with this activity. You may choose to use these to support all the children in the class, or only those children who need extra support.

If you wish to do a teacher introduction we suggest that you take the opportunity to do a shared rereading of the story opening on pages 18 and 19 and emphasize main structural features of a story – characters, setting, plot and the chronological order of events (who? when? where? what?).

### ASSESSMENT POINTS

As the children work you may wish to observe whether and to what degree they can do the following:

#### Plan
- order events chronologically
- choose appropriate adjectives to describe a character
- write a detailed description of a setting
- produce a beginning, middle and end plan

#### First draft
- write a first draft with an appropriate introductory sentence, events arranged chronologically and suitable ending
- use adjectives to describe characters and setting

#### Revise
- read text through to another child
- comment on the content and/or structure of the passage with questions as guidance

#### Edit
- locate his/her own spelling, grammar and punctuation mistakes

#### Final draft
- set out a story legibly

Unit 2

**Teacher's observations: descriptions of characters**

This is quite a detailed description using appropriate adjectives. The writer obviously draws on his own experience. The spelling is irregular, but in logical ways. Some sentences are not punctuated appropriately. The writer has used both past and present tense. Reading through this piece would bring some of these issues to the child's attention.

**Teacher's observations: descriptions of setting**

The description radiates enthusiasm, using appropriate adjectives to offer a detailed description. The sentences are generally will defined, although the number of 'ands' could be reduced by making more sentences. The spelling is not completely accurate, but the errors are mostly uncommon words (for this child) and are logically made. The plural of deer is incorrect, although sheep is correct.

# Descriptions of characters

Rory is about my age and he has got a cold. He is 7. He has got red hair and a red nose and I think he is called carotts at schoo by his frends. He was wereing a stripey top it is a football top. So he likes football. He has got a funny face with very big eyes.

# Descriptions of setting

The park is very big. It has got two main parts. One is where the animas are. There are real deers, wooly sheep and a pets corner with rabbits. The best bit of the park is the swings and there are roundabouts and slides too. They are new and have just been bilt and is all brit colouts.

## Plan

| The beginning – | |
|---|---|
| character | Rory |
| setting | At home |
| First event | Goes out.<br>Mum said take your coat.<br>Rory does not take it.<br>Gos to the park |
| Middle | A massive storm<br>Other kids have coats.<br>Rory gets soked. |
| End | cold he sneeses<br>Has to stay in bed |

Plan: good structuring of events and a full understanding of the picture story. There is no indication about the character other than actions. A wide range of vocabulary has been used. Although some of the words are incorrectly spelt, this can be corrected later. Some changes in tense also needs attention.

# UNIT 2 Writing to entertain – story

Name _____ Group _____ Date _____

| ASSESSMENT POINT<br>*Can the child:* | PB page or PCM | | | |
|---|---|---|---|---|
| **Text level** | | | | |
| read and understand a narrative opening | 18–19 | | | |
| plan *character*, *setting* and *events* using charts, descriptions and flowchart | 30–31<br>PCMs 17–19, 37 | | | |
| *draft* from planning notes | 30–31<br>PCM 38 | | | |
| discuss and revise a story | 31 | | | |
| produce a final draft with appropriate punctuation and grammar | 31 | | | |
| answer literal and inferential comprehension questions | 20 | | | |
| order events in chronological order | 28 | | | |
| recognize the structural features of a narrative of a narrative opening (*introduction, events, characters, settings*) | 18–19 | | | |
| recognize and write *direct speech* where appropriate | 29 | | | |
| differentiate the purpose and features of *fiction* and *non-fiction* texts | 26–27 | | | |
| differentiate diagrams and their purposes | 27 | | | |
| **Sentence level** | 1 2 | | | |
| recognize and use *verbs* in sentences | 24<br>PCM 12 | | | |
| understand past and present and use *tense* to indicate in sentences | 25<br>PCM 13 | | | |
| recognize and use *adjectives* in sentences to write descriptions | 22<br>PCM 10 | | | |
| recognize and write *similes* | 23 | | | |
| identify and write *direct speech* in *speech bubbles* | 29 | | | |
| write direct speech in *speech marks* | 29<br>PCM 16 | | | |
| **Word level** | | | | |
| recognize and use homophones | 28<br>PCM 15 | | | |
| know and write the *seasons* and *months* of the year and set out *dates* | 21<br>PCM 9 | | | |

*Unit 2*

# Months and seasons

Name _____ Date _____

May
March
December
July
January
February

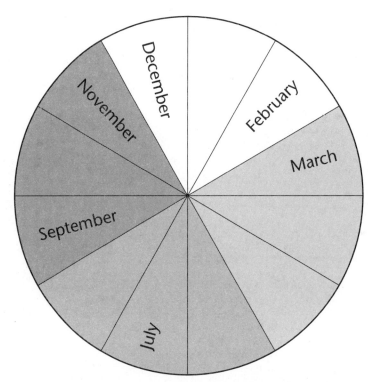

August
October
September
April
November
June

**1** Write in the names of the missing months.

  **a** The months of spring are _____ , _____

  and _____ .

  **b** The months of summer are _____ ,

  _____ and _____ .

  **c** The months of autumn are _____ ,

  and _____ .

  **d** The months of winter are _____ , _____

  and _____ .

  **e** The months of the year start with capital letters.

**2** Fill in the missing details from this sentence.

  My birthday is on _____ . *month*

  It is in the _____ . *day* *season*

© OUP: This page may be reproduced for class use solely within the purchaser's school or college

# Adjectives

Name _____ Date _____

This account has only got one adjective – 'nice'.
Make it more interesting by replacing 'nice' with
different adjectives

It was a ~~nice~~ day. A ~~nice~~ sun was shining and
the sky had a few ~~nice~~ clouds. A ~~nice~~ dog ran
along a ~~nice~~ road. He ran past the ~~nice~~ man
and the ~~nice~~ girl. He ran under the ~~nice~~ shade of
a ~~nice~~ tree and into the ~~nice~~ park. He had seen a
~~nice~~ cat. The ~~nice~~ cat got ready to run away.
She did not like the ~~nice~~ dog. She climbed up a
~~nice~~ tree next to a ~~nice~~ pond.

# Descriptions

Name _____ Date _____

Reread the passage and look at the pictures on pages 18 and 19 of the pupil's book. The tree is described at different seasons of the year.

**1** Fill in the chart below. Some of the entries are done for you.

| Season | What the tree looked like | What William did | What happened to the tree |
|---|---|---|---|
| **Spring** | Like a pale green umbrella with lots of new leaves. | Looked up at the birds building their nests. | The leaves started to grow. |
| **Summer** | | | |
| **Autumn** | | | |
| **Winter** | | | |

# *Verbs*

Name_____  Date_____

**1** Draw a picture of someone doing each of these activities. Make each picture about the same person.

| sleeping | eating | playing | reading |
|---|---|---|---|

**2** Now write a short story about the person based on your four pictures.

_____

_____

_____

_____

_____

_____

_____

_____

_____

_____

**3** When you have finished the story go through and underline a verb in each sentence.

# Tense

Name _____     Date _____

**Monday**          **Wednesday**          **Friday**

**1** It is now Saturday. Write to your Gran telling her what you have done during the week.

Saturday morning

Dear Gran,

    I have had an exciting week. On Monday evening I

_____

_____

_____

_____

_____

_____

_____

_____

**2** Now go through your writing and underline all the verbs that say what you have already done. These are verbs in the past tense.

# Fiction and non-fiction

Name _____ Date _____

**1** Look at these book covers. They are both books about clothes.

a

b

**2** Decide which book is fiction and which is non-fiction. Give one reason why you think this.

**a** I think book a is a _____ book because _____ . . . . . . . .

............... . . . . . . . . . .

**b** I think book b is a _____ book because _____ . . . . . . . .

............... . . . . . . . . . .

# Homophones

Name _____ Date _____

## Whether

Whether the weather be fine
Or whether the weather be not
Whether the weather be cold
Or whether the weather be hot –
We'll weather the weather
Whatever the weather
Whether we like it or not.

*Anon*

Write out this passage and decide which is the correct word from each pair of words.

The son/sun was shining as Sammy walked down the rode/road. He could see/sea a rain cloud ahead. 'I wonder weather/whether I'll get home before it starts to rain/reign,' he thought. 'Oh no/know! I can hear/here thunder.' Sammy began to/two run. 'Eye/I will get home in time,' he thought. But the rain caught/court up with him. It was no good. He got soaked. 'What dreadful (weather, whether),' said his mum. 'You need/knead to take a coat next time you/yew go out.'

# *Direct speech*

Name _____ Date _____

**1** Read this story.

**2** What the people actually say is in the bubbles. Write this as a story and put the things the people say in the story into speech marks. The story is started for you.

### An early breakfast

Mum called 'Tea's ready, Chris.' But as she stepped into the room, a football knocked the tray out of her hands. ' _____ ' yelled Chris, but it was too late. Mum dropped things everywhere!

' _____ ,' shouted Mum. So Chris went to bed early.

In the night _____

_____

_____

_____ .

# *Story plan 1*

Name _____ Date _____

| | |
|---|---|
| **The beginning** | |
| **character** (who?) | |
| **setting** (when and where?) | |
| **First event** (what?) | |
| **Middle** (what happens next?) | |
| **The ending** | |

# *Story plan 2*

Name ................................................ Date ................................

| Title | |
|---|---|
| Orientation | |
| Characters | |
| Setting | |
| Events | |
| Problem | |
| Resolution | |
| Conclusion | |

# A character web

Name _____ Date _____

| Looks like ... | Sounds like ... |

**Name of character**

_____

| Feels ... | Does ... |

# Writing to express

| Pupils' Book content | Whole class | Teacher led | Independent | PCM |
|---|---|---|---|---|
| **Texts** | | | | |
| poems | 33, 38–39 | 33, 38–39 | 34 | |
| limericks | | | 43 | |
| nursery rhymes | | 36 | | 23 |
| rhyming couplets | | | 37 | |
| jokes | 38–39 | 38–39 | 42 | |
| **Text features** | | | | |
| rhyme | 33,38–39 | 33, 38–39 | 34, 43, 45 | 21 |
| rhythm | 38–39 | 38–39 | 43 | |
| **Reading skills** | | | | |
| literal and inferential | 38–39 | | 34, 38 | |
| **Writing skills** | | | | |
| writing sentences | 39 | | 37, 39 | |
| writing couplets | | | 37 | |
| writing limericks | | | 43 | |
| planning verse | 44–45 | | 44–45 | |
| drafting a verse | 44–45 | | 44–45 | 38 |
| writing nursery rhymes | | | | 23 |
| working riddles | | | | 24 |
| **Grammar** | | | | |
| sentences | 39 | | 37, 39 | 45 |
| verbs | | | 35, 37 | |
| a or an | | | 35 | |
| proper nouns | | | 43 | |
| direct speech | 36 | 36 | | |
| **Punctuation** | | | | |
| question marks | | | 39 | 24 |
| capital letters | | | 43 | |
| **Words** | | | | |
| rhyming words | 33 | 33 | 45 | 21 |
| vowels consonants | | | 35 | 22 |
| question words | | 39 | 39 | 24 |
| onomatopoeia | | | 40 | |
| contradictions | 41 | 41 | | |
| homographs | | | 42 | |
| shortened words | | | 42 | |
| paired words | | | 34 | 20 |
| time words | 41 | 41 | | 25 |

LEAD LESSON

# Writing to express

## Aims of the lead lesson

- to read a poem and understand the content
- to discuss how the author uses language creatively and effectively in a poem
- to explore the structure and language features of a simple poem
- to examine the layout and punctuation conventions of a simple poem

---

| SESSION 1 | *Introducing the text* |

*pen a*

### Content and meaning

- Explain that you are going to read, enjoy and look closely at a poem.
- Draw the children's attention to the demonstration poster. (Have just the title and author visible, the rest of the text masked.)
- Explain that this is a large version of the poem on the opening pages of Unit 3 (pages 32–33) in the Pupils' Book. (DO NOT ask them to look at the poem in their books yet.)
- Give the title and the author's name. Highlight this information on the poster. Ask the children to predict what they think the poem might be about.
- Reveal and read the first line. What does this make them think? It might remind them of other refrains. It is not a very serious opening. Uncover and read the whole poem to the class.
- Reread the demonstration text with the children following the text in their books. Check their understanding of the content by questioning. Are these things they would really do? Why is the poem funny? Do these foods really exist?

# Writing to express

## Did You Really? —————— *title*

*How do the first lines catch your interest?*

*Dip, dip, dip!* —————— *Does this first line remind you of another poem?*

Did you ever lick

a lollipop stick

dipped into the mustard?

*Did it make you sick?* —————— *How does each verse end? What do you notice about the type of print?*

*My, my, my!* ——————

Did you ever try ——————  *What do you notice about these words?*

a popcorn pie ——————

*What is popcorn pie?* —————— chopped up with an onion?

*Did it make you cry?* ——————

{ *Hoo, hoo, hoo!* —————— *Is there a pattern to the punctuation? Why?*
{ Did you ever chew
{ a bubble-gum stew
{ mixed up with custard?
*a verse* —————— { *Can I have some too?*

by *Judith Nicholls*

*author* ——————

| Key | | | | | |
|---|---|---|---|---|---|
| *pen a* | Content or words to look up | *pen b* | Text features | *pen c* | Sentence and word features |

*pen b* ᔕᔕᔕ

## SESSION 2 | *Analysing the lead text*

### Text level features

- If starting a whole class session at this point reread the text with the class in an appropriate way. Either read it to the class or select children to read verses.

- Ask how the poem is divided up (use the term 'verses'). Annotate verses with numbers: 1, 2, 3.

- Ask how each verse begins. Why do they think each verse opens like this?

- Ask how each verse ends. (With a question.) Point out that each verse consists of an opening refrain, main question and closing question. How is the final question different from the other two? (The first two questions are to people who have eaten the stuff and how it felt ['you']; the last question involves the author ['I'].)

- Ask what they notice about the font (typeface). The opening and closing lines are in italic. Again, this helps make verse structure clear.

PB pages 32–33

## SESSION 3 | *Analysing the lead text*

*pen c* ᴧᴧᴧᴧᴧᴧ

### Sentence and word level features

- If starting a third whole-class session at this point reread the poem with the class in an appropriate way. Either read it together or select children to read verses.

- Ask the children to identify the end rhymes in each verse. Point out that rhyme is about the sound of the word not the spelling of the word.

- Underline the rhymes in each verse. Is there a pattern to the rhymes? What is the effect of the fourth line not rhyming? (Makes that word stand out, emphasizes its importance.)

- As well as rhyme, poets use words in other ways to make us notice them more. Can the children see anywhere where the poet has used

  – repetition of words

  – alliteration (where sounds are repeated).

- Underline and annotate. These are all ways of stressing individual words.

- Point out punctuation and its function. (Exclamation marks indicate surprise and give clues as to expression when reading aloud. Questions marks do the same. You would put a query into your voice if reading aloud.)

- Finally, reread the poem for all to enjoy.

## Related activities

**PCM 20**
**TG page 76**

- PCM 20 (More silly foods) is a word level activity about anagrams.
- Ask the children to find other poems that have opening refrains and start a class 'wall of poems'. (This could be used as a handwriting activity.)

**PB page 34**

# Using words

**Text and word level**

## Aims

- to answer literal and inferential questions
- to understand that rhyme is based on sound

## Teaching notes

Children should be able to do this work in 20 minutes without assistance. However, for some groups it will be useful to start with a group reading of the poem (on page 33).

---

**ANSWERS**

1 **a** mustard  **b** popcorn pie  **c** bubble-gum stew
2 jelly and ice cream, fish and chips, bread and jam, curry and rice
4 rhymes left in the poem: stick, sick/my, pie, cry/chew, stew

---

## Related activities

- Make a collection of nonsense verse for the class. Shorter nonsense poems can be used for handwriting practice. It is also fun for children to learn short poems by heart, perhaps as a homework activity. The child can then recite the poem to the class and pick out rhymes.

**PCM 21**
**TG page 77**

- PCM 21 (Rhymes) gives further practice at recognizing rhymes.

# Verbs

Sentence and word level

## Aims

- to look at alternatives for particular verbs
- to distinguish vowels and consonants
- to use the indefinite article appropriately

## Teaching notes

Verbs for actions have been introduced in Units 1 and 2. This activity concentrates on suitability in sentences.

Many children can use the indefinite article ('a' or 'an') correctly in speech. This activity makes the 'rule' explicit so that you can discuss it when errors occur in children's work. If children are unclear about vowels and consonants, it may be a good idea to focus on this in whole-class word-study time.

### ANSWERS

1 sucked, gobbled, chewed, nibbled

2 **a** an, a     **b** an, an

PCM 22
TG page 78

## Related activities

- PCM 22 (Vowels and consonants)
- Children can go through the page of a book, newspaper article, etc. noting 'a' and 'an'. Make a list of these with the word that follows. Which begin with a consonant, which with a vowel?

## Speech in bubbles

Sentence level

## Aims

- to identify direct speech in a text
- to identify the pattern of rhymes in a poem

## Teaching notes

Read the poem and discuss the rhyme pattern with the pupils. Remind them of the rhyme pattern of the opening poem. Ask the children to read the poem aloud with individuals taking the parts of the narrator, old woman and giant as a way of revisiting direct speech.

### ANSWERS

1 **a** giant: What can I do? My foot it has blisters. I can't hardly walk.
  **b** old woman: HOP IT! I've no time to talk.

2 **a** What! Lost your mittens? You naughty kittens! Then you shall have no pie.
  **b** Oh, mother dear, we sadly fear that we have lost our mittens.

## Related activities

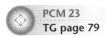

**PCM 23**
**TG page 79**

- Ask the children to complete cartoon strips with empty bubbles.
- Ask the children to turn well-known stories, e.g. Goldilocks, into cartoon strips, telling most of the story through speech bubbles.
- PCM 23 (New nursery rhymes) gives children practice at inventing nursery rhymes.

*PB page 37*

# Rhyming couplets

Word level

## Aims

- to look at further rhyming patterns
- to look at alternatives for common verbs

## Teaching notes

The alternative verbs are not synonyms, because they do not mean exactly the same thing. The best way to find alternative words is to use a thesaurus. Introduce this to the children by modelling exactly how you look up 'said' and making a list of alternatives they might use. Discuss the differences in meaning between examples, e.g. muttered, barked, shouted, said.

## Related activities

- Ask the children to collect and list alternative words for 'eating', 'drinking' and 'breathing', using the thesaurus.

- Use the poem 'Mrs Armitage on Wheels' by Quentin Blake. Replace 'said' in the 'said Mrs Armitage' refrain used throughout the book with an alternative word.

PB pages 38–39

# Question poems

Text and word level

## Aims

- to explore rhyme patterns further
- to practise literal and inferential comprehension
- to use question words and question marks

## Teaching notes

Use the poems on these pages as a whole-class shared reading or for guided reading. This will ensure that all the children have read the poems carefully and give you the chance to emphasize rhyming couplets and punchlines.

PCM 24
TG page 80

## Related activities

- PCM 24 (Riddles) gives children practice in solving and making up their own riddles.
- Ask children to write riddles ending 'Who am I?' or 'What am I?'

PB page 40

# Noisy words

Word level

## Aims

- to explore the impact of onomatopoeia
- to examine the impact of font/visual representation on words

## Teaching notes

At this age it is not important that children know the term 'onomatopoeia' (let alone spell it!), they simply need to relate the sound of the word to the sound it describes.

### ANSWERS

1 hen/cluck, dog/bark, cat/purr, horse/neigh, sheep/baa, blackbird/sing, wolf/howl

## Related activities

- Ask children to look through comics, magazines and picture books for examples of words which are set out in a very visual way or which represent a sound.
- Make a collection of different examples. Discuss why, when and where they were used.

PB page 41

# What nonsense!

Text level

## Aims

- to recognize contradictions and their role in humour
- to use time words

Unit 3

## Teaching notes

Time words are important for structuring chronological writing and for helping the reader understand texts. A shared or guided reading of a text containing time words can be used as a basis for discussion of this.

> **ANSWERS**
>
> 2 'Went' is the past tense, while 'tomorrow' indicates the future.
> 3  **a** This morning *or* today     **c** yesterday
>     **b** last year     **d** next week *or* tomorrow *or* next month

## Related activity

PCM 25
TG page 81

■ PCM 25 (Calendar/time words) gives children practice in naming the days of the week and months of the year.

PB page 42

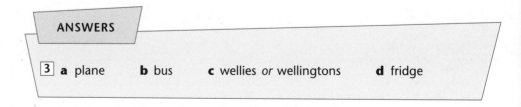
# The same but different

Word level

## Aims

■ to examine homographs to show their different meanings
■ to be aware of word change

## Teaching notes

Homographs are words which have the same form and sound, but a different meaning ('calf' and 'calf'). Homophones have the same sound but different forms and different meanings ('there' and 'their').

> **ANSWERS**
>
> 3  **a** plane     **b** bus     **c** wellies *or* wellingtons     **d** fridge

## Related activity

PCM 26
TG page 82

■ PCM 26 (Homographs) is a further activity about homographs.

# Limericks

Text and sentence level

## Aims

■ to introduce limericks and their rhyme pattern

■ to use capital letters in place names

## Teaching notes

Limericks have five lines with a traditional syllable pattern of 8, 8, 6, 6, 8. You could investigate this with children by clapping the limerick and putting a mark on a board (or flipchart) for each beat. Some limericks repeat line 1 in line 5.

The five lines of a limerick also have an A-A-B-B-A rhyme scheme. This is another feature to pick out. The poem on this page could be used for shared or guided reading followed by examination of rhythm and rhyme patterns.

Although place names as proper nouns are introduced here, the term 'proper nouns' has not been used.

### ANSWERS

1 a Wales    b Wight    c France

# Writing a funny verse

## Aims

■ to choose themes for verses of a nursery rhyme

■ to write a poem with appropriate rhymes

■ to plan using a brainstorm web and sentences

■ to draft and revise a poem

## Teaching notes

This activity draws together the skills used in Unit 3 so that the children can use them to write a simple poem. The activity can be done in one long session or as a number of shorter sessions. Doing the activity as a number of shorter sessions offers you the chance to use both products (drafts, notes, etc.) and observation for assessment purposes.

If you wish to do a teacher introduction we suggest that you take the opportunity to do a shared reading of 'Old Mother Hubbard' and remind the class about the main structural features of a poem, including rhyme, opening verse, repetition, and brevity of lines.

---

**ASSESSMENT POINTS**

As you observe children working, you may wish to bear in mind to what extent children can do the following:

**Plan**

- choose an appropriate shop to write about
- make a general web of ideas and add detail to it

**First draft**

- write a first draft with an appropriate starting sentence, rhyme pattern and words

**Revise**

- read text through to another child
- comment on the content and/or structure of the poem with questions as guidance

**Edit**

- locate his/her own spelling, grammar and punctuation mistakes

**Final draft**

- set out a poem appropriately with a capital letter at the start of each line

---

skirt               hat

**DRESS SHOP**

t-shirt          scarf

---

comic

book                  paper

**BOOK SHOP**

tape                  video

---

**Teacher's observation**

There are a number of good, relevant ideas here. The spelling and transcription are unimportant in notes, but all these are correct.

---

First draft

She went to the dress shop to buy him a skirt
But wen he got back he was wering a shirt

She went to the book shop to buy him a book
But when she got back he shouted O look

---

This draft is a good effort. The child has used rhyme very successfully and included capital letters at the start of each line. The ideas reflect the notes in the brainstorm web.

In the final draft the child needs to set these verses out like the original used for shared reading. A look at the poster will help. The child can consider where the full stops and capital letters should go. Suggesting a full stop after each idea might help.

---

# UNIT 3 Writing to express – humorous poems

Name _____ Group _____ Date _____

| ASSESSMENT POINT<br>Can the child: | PB page or PCM | Comments |
|---|---|---|
| **Text level** | | |
| *read* and understand a poem | 33, 36, 37, 38,<br>39, 41, 43<br>PCM 23 | |
| select ideas for verses using a *brainstorming web* | 44–45 | |
| *draft* from planning notes | 44–45 | |
| discuss and *revise* additional verses of a familiar poem | 45<br>PCM 23 | |
| produce a *final draft* with appropriate punctuation | 45 | |
| answer literal and inferential comprehension questions | 34, 38, 39 | |
| recognize features of a poem (*onomatopoeia, repetition, alliteration, rhyme*) | 32, 33, 38, 39 | |
| **Sentence level** | | |
| recognize and complete questions | 39 | |
| recognize and complete sentences | 37, 39 | |
| use *capital letters* at the start of a line | 32, 33, 43 | |
| use *capital letters* for names | 43 | |
| recognize *verbs* and appreciate the effects on a sentence of changing verbs | 35, 37 | |
| recognize direct speech | 36 | |
| use appropriate indefinite article (a or an) with *consonants* or *vowels* | 35 | |
| **Word level** | | |
| recognize the *rhythm* of a poem | 38, 39, 43 | |
| recognize and use words which indicate time | 41<br>PCM 25 | |
| use wh– question words | 39<br>PCM 24 | |
| select words and combinations of words for humerous effects | 37, 43, 45 | |
| homographs | 42<br>PCM 26 | |
| pick out *rhymes* and rhyme patterns | 33, 34, 38,<br>39, 43, 45<br>PCM 21 | |
| know *consonants* and *vowels* | 35<br>PCM 22 | |
| identify and write *onomatopoeia* | 40 | |
| identify rhymes | 34<br>PCM 21 | |

# *More silly foods*

Name _____    Date _____

**1** The labels to these foods are jumbled up. Write
them out correctly. The first one is done for you.
Then check your spellings in a dictionary.

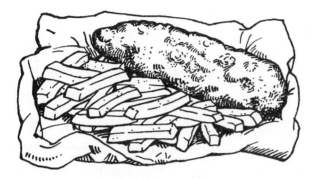

shif dna spchi

fish and chips

maj wisahndc

............................................

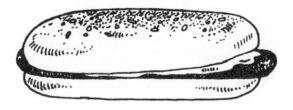

hto dgo

............................................

aaannb nad eci-raemc

............................................

radeb dan esehce

............................................

# Rhymes

Name ........................................................... Date .................................

**1** Find the words in the box that rhyme with the pictures, and write them in.

| | | | | | | |
|---|---|---|---|---|---|---|
| hop | shop | hum | yum | drop | worn | born |
| | sum | mum | torn | top | rum | horn |

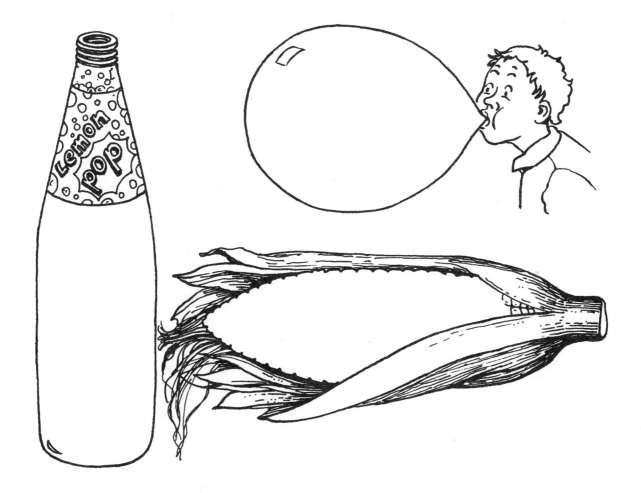

**2** Can you find rhyming words for these food words?

jam        meat

.......................   .......................

.......................   .......................

.......................   .......................

.......................   .......................

# Vowels and consonants

Name _____  Date _____

1 Fill in the missing letters on the alphabet snake.

2 Colour in the five steps that contain the vowels (a e i o u).

The letters you have left are all consonants.

The toy shop below has lost some letters from its labels.

If the missing letter is marked C it is a consonant

If the missing letter is marked V it is a vowel.

3 Write the correct labels.

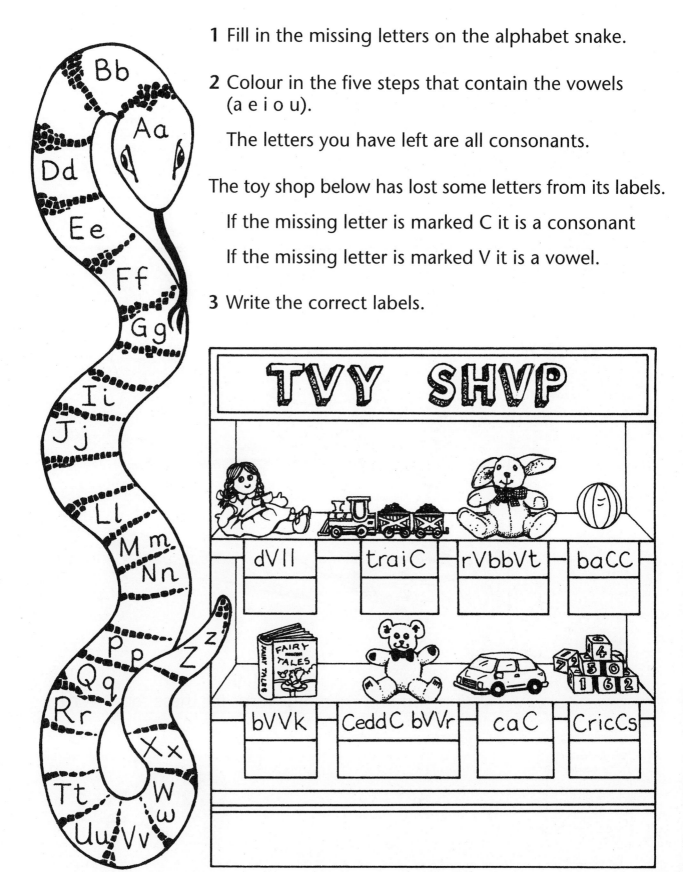

© OUP: This page may be reproduced for class use solely within the purchaser's school or college

# New nursery rhymes

Name _____  Date _____

Here are some more versions of well-known rhymes.

> Georgie Porgie Candy Floss
> Kissed the girls and made them cross;
> When the boys came out to play,
> The ambulance took George away.
> *by Colin McNaughton*

> Twinkle twinkle little bat!
> How I wonder what you're at!
> Up above the world you fly
> Like a tea-tray in the sky.
> *by Lewis Carroll*

> Pussycat, pussycat, where have you been
> Licking your lips with your whiskers
>      so clean?
> Pussycat, pussycat, purring and pudgy
> Pussycat, pussycat. WHERE IS OUR
>      BUDGIE?
> *by Max Fatchen*

**1** Make up your own version of a nursery rhyme, starting with one of these well-known lines.

**a** Humpty Dumpty sat on a _____
Humpty Dumpty had _____

**b** To market to market to buy a _____
Home again, home again _____

**c** Mary had a little _____
Its _____

**d** Hickory dickory _____
The mouse ran up the _____

**2** After you have written your rhyme draw a picture to go with it.

# Riddles

Name _____ Date _____

**1** Can you solve these riddles? Draw what you think each one is.

> I have four legs
> I wag my tail
> I bark
> What am I?

> I am round
> I am orange
> People eat me
> What am I?

> I have four legs,
> One back and one seat.
> What am I?

> I am round
> I am yellow
> I shine in the sky
> What am I?

**2** Now make up your own riddles for these objects.

 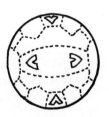 

.................................... .................................... ....................................

.................................... .................................... ....................................

.................................... .................................... ....................................

.................................... .................................... ....................................

**3** Choose something to make up a riddle about. See if other people can solve it.

# *Calendar/time words*

Name _____ Date _____

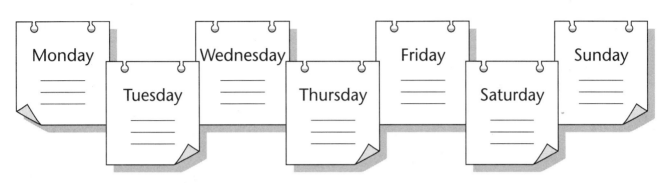

**1** Finish off these sentences about the days of the week.

**a** Yesterday was Wednesday so today is _____ .

**b** Today is Friday so tomorrow will be _____ .

**c** Tomorrow is Tuesday. Today is _____ .

**d** Today is Monday. I am going swimming the day after tomorrow.

   So I am going on _____ .

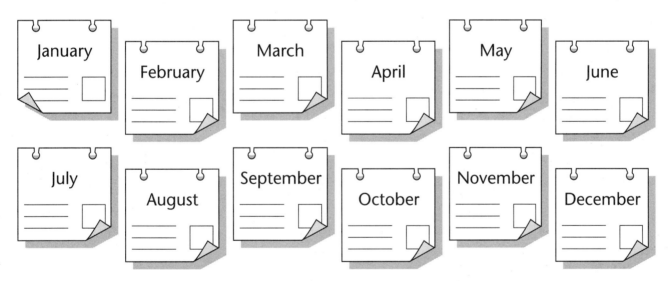

**2** Now finish off these sentences about the months of the year.

**a** This month is _____ .

**b** Next month will be _____ .

**c** Last month was _____ .

**d** My birthday is in _____ .

# *Homographs*

Name _____ Date _____

**1** Fill in the missing words. The same word goes in two of the sentences but they mean different things in each sentence.

    **a** Simple Simon met a pie man going to the _____ .

       'It's not _____ ,' she said.

    **b** The car had a _____ tyre.

       I live in a _____ .

    **c** She got all her sums _____ .

       Turn _____ to get to the shops.

    **d** The _____ was caught in the spiders web.

       Peter Pan was a boy who could _____ .

**2** Make up two sentences for each of these words. In each sentence give the word a different meaning.

left       watch       note

# Writing to report

| Pupils' Book content | Whole class  | Teacher led  | Independent  | PCM  |
|---|---|---|---|---|
| **Texts** | | | | |
| non-chronological report | 40–47 | 46–47 | | 27 |
| invitations | | | 50 | 29 |
| descriptions | 55 | 55 | 51, 52–53 | |
| charts | 54–55 | 54–55 | | |
| **Text features** | | | | |
| opening definition | 46–47 | 46–47 | | 27 |
| logically order paragraphs | 46–47 | 46–47 | | 27 |
| photographs | 46–47 | 46–47 | | |
| captions | 46–47 | 46–47 | | |
| **Reading skills** | | | | |
| literal and inferential comprehension | 55 | 55 | 48, 50 | 29 |
| extracting information from visual sources | | | 49 | 29 |
| **Writing skills** | | | | |
| writing sentences | 57, 58–59 | 57 | 48, 58–59 | 34 |
| descriptions | | 55 | 51, 52–53 | |
| brainstorming ideas | 58 | | 58 | |
| planning a report | | | 58 | |
| drafting a report | | | 59 | |
| revising a report | | | 59 | 38 |
| **Grammar** | | | | |
| sentences | 57, 58–59 | | 48 | 34 |
| the verb 'to be' | | | 48 | |
| adjectives | | | 51, 52 | 30 |
| **Punctuation** | | | | |
| exclamation marks | 56 | 56 | | |
| commas in lists | 57 | 57 | | 34 |
| **Words** | | | | |
| days of the week | | | 49 | 28 |
| singular and plural nouns | | | 52 | 31 |
| alphabetical order | | | 53 | 32 |
| months | 55 | 55 | 55 | 33 |

# Writing to report

## Aims of the lead lesson

- to identify the purpose and possible audience for which this report was written
- to read and understand the content of the report
- to explore the structural features of a written report (opening classification or definition, non-chronological sequence)
- to identify the language features of a report (present tense, technical vocabulary, verbs, verb 'to be') – to demonstrate that details may be added using pictures as well as text

| SESSION 1 | *Introducing the text* |

*pen a*

### Content and meaning

This lesson looks at how reports work, using an example report on festivals and celebrations.

- Draw the children's attention to the demonstration poster and explain that this is a large version of the report on the opening pages of Unit 4 (pages 46–47) in the Pupils' Book. Explain that you are going to look at how we write when we want to inform others about something
- Pick out the title and ask the children to find this in their books. After looking at the title and quickly looking at (skimming) the rest of the page, what do they think the report will be about?
- Read the extract aloud. As you read each section also draw the children's attention to the photographs and read the caption where one exists. Do not comment on the purpose of the pictures at this point.
- Reread the demonstration text with the children following the text in their books. Check their understanding of the content by questioning: What are festivals and celebrations? Festivals can be divided into different kinds depending on why they are held. What reasons for holding celebrations are given? Are festivals universal or specific to one country?
- Annotate any unknown words, e.g. Divali, Hanuka and Eid-Ul-Fitr, and demonstrate how to look them up in a dictionary.

## SESSION 2 | *Analysing the lead text*

*pen b* ~~~~~~

### Text level features

- If starting a whole-class session at this point revisit the text with the class either by reading it to them or selecting children to read paragraphs.

- Ask the children to find the opening sentence. Reread and underline. What does this first sentence do? (The beginning of a report usually gives a general definition of what is being talked about.) Annotate with 'general opening definition'.

- Reread the next two sentences. What do these sentences do? (They say more about festivals but again they give general information that could apply to *any* festival.) Annotate with 'more general information'.

- Look at the photograph of the birthday party and read the caption below it. How is this information different from the opening information? (It is now beginning to talk about *specific* festivals rather than *all* festivals.) Annotate with 'specific types of festivals'.

- What does the photograph do? Annotate with 'adds more details'.

- Ask whether it matters if paragraphs 2, 3 and 4 (different types of festivals) are printed in this order. Would it alter the meaning if the order was different? Emphasize that as writing is not in chronological order, the order of these paragraphas could be changed. As long as all the details about each kind of festival are together, the order on the page does not matter. In some writing, the order *does* matter, e.g. retelling events, giving instructions.

- Who is this text written for? Is anybody mentioned by name? Who is the text written about? Is anybody mentioned by name? Explain that report-writing is often impersonal. It is written to be read by lots of people and it talks about general things. This concept of personal/impersonal tone and generic participants rather than personal participants is difficult for children of this age. The aim here is merely to begin to draw their attention to these factors. They are developed more fully in later levels.

## SESSION 3 | *Analysing the lead text*

*pen c* ∧∧∧∧∧

### Sentence and word level features

- If starting a whole-class session at this point, revisit the text with the class either by reading it to them or selecting children to read paragraphs.

- The report contains verbs telling us what people do at festival times. Ask the children to identify some of these and underline them, e.g. wear, eat, give. What is the tense of these verbs? Annotate with 'present tense'.

**OXFORD LITERACY WEB**     Launch into Literacy, Foundation Book, Unit 4

*Unit 4*

# Writing to report

*title*

## Festivals and Celebrations

*An opening general definition*

*verbs in the present tense*

Festivals and celebrations are special events which mark important days. During celebrations people often wear special clothes, eat special foods and give each other cards and presents. Sometimes they decorate their houses too.

*more genera information*

*a particular festival*

There are festivals for important days in people's lives like birthdays, weddings and anniversaries.

**Key**

*pen a*  Content or words to look up     *pen b*  Text features     *pen c*  Sentence and word features

# OXFORD LITERACY WEB

Launch into Literacy, Foundation Book, Unit 4

## Writing to report (continued)

*Unit 4*

*part of the verb 'to be'*

There are special celebrations to mark important times of the year like harvest and New Year.

*more information on particular festivals in the pictures and captions*

🎉 *Chinese New Year celebrations*

There are religious celebrations such as Christmas, Divali, Hanuka and Eid-Ul-Fitr. These special days remind people of important times in their <u>religions.</u>

🎉 *Thanksgiving Day dinner*

*no-one mentioned by name*

*check meaning*

There are also special days to remind people of the <u>important</u> things that happened in their country like Thanksgiving Day in America and Independence Day in India.

**Key**

*pen a* <u>Content or words to look up</u>    *pen b* Text features    *pen c* Sentence and word features

- Many of the sentences start with the same words. What are they? Underline 'There are'. Explain that 'are' is part of the verb 'to be' – a very important verb which changes depending on who the sentence is about. 'I am', 'you are', 'it is' are all part of the verb 'to be'.

- Briefly recap the whole session or the three shorter sessions. Reports inform us about things by giving us a definition and then going into more detail about what is being described. They are usually impersonal and written in the present tense.

## Plenary session

Use the questions above or those in the Pupils' Book to examine the children's understanding of the content, structure and language features of the report they have studied

## Related activity

**PCM 27**
**TG page 98**

- Use PCM 27 (Celebration cards) to check the children's understanding of how a report is structured (opening definition, general details, characteristics relating to the object being described). PCM 27 is a jumbled-up report text which needs sequencing. In order to undertake this, pupils will need to draw on their understanding of how reports are structured, as well as using syntactic and semantic clues.

**PB page 48**

# Festivals and celebrations

**Text level**

## Aims

- to answer literal and inferential comprehension questions
- to complete sentences
- to develop knowledge of the verb 'to be'

## Teaching notes

Remind the children about the various forms of the verb 'to be' and of how it changes form depending upon the subject of the verb.

## Related activity

- Give the children copies of a familiar text and ask them to identify and underline any examples they find of the verb 'to be'. With more able children you could also ask them to identify whether the verb indicates the present or the past.

PB page 49

# Celebration cards

Text and word level

## Aims

- to use visual information for comprehension
- to identify days of the week

## Teaching notes

Children are used to using the visual information in picture books to support their reading. This page makes explicit the use of visual as well as written clues. You may feel it useful to discuss with the class or group why certain symbols are associated with particular celebrations.

**PCM 28**
**TG page 99**

## Related activities

- PCM 28 (Days of the week) gives further practice naming days of the week.
- Ask the children to make a chart of daily events in their lives, e.g. Monday: swimming, Brownies; Tuesday: visit Gran, etc. Then have them create 'Solomon Grundy' rhymes using their own names:

  e.g. Sally Brown
  Goes swimming on Monday, (etc.)

PB page 50

# Writing invitations

Text level

## Aims

- to answer literal and inferential comprehension questions
- to write an invitation

## Teaching notes

As well as asking children to select very precise information from an invitation, this activity focuses on how invitations are set out. The children do their own invitations generalizing the 'rules' from the example given. When correcting work or offering support, use the example for reference.

**ANSWERS**

1. a Rashida
   b Rashida's birthday
   c 7 years old
   d Yes. Sally can come to the party.

## Related activities

- PCM 29 (Rebus invitations)
- Ask the children to create further invitations based on well known stories, e.g. A ball invitation for the Cinderella story.
- Collect examples of a range of birthday party invitations. Compare these looking at language, what is always included, designs/layout, degrees of formality, etc.

**PCM 29**
**TG page 100**

# Using adjectives

Sentence level

## Aim
■ to recognize and use adjectives

## Teaching notes
This activity concentrates upon adjectives of quality.

### ANSWERS

1 There are several adjectives which would make sense, including:
   **a** big, lovely, nice, gorgeous, huge, delicious
   **b** interesting, beautiful, fascinating, lovely
2 Other adjectives may be used as long as they make sense within the context.
   **a** Rashida had a big, brown, cuddly teddy bear.
   **b** She got a round, bouncy, black and white football.
   **c** She was given a long, spotted, woollen scarf.

## Related activities
■ Ask children to write precise descriptions of favourite possessions.
■ PCM 30 (Describing toys) is a further activity using adjectives.

PCM 30
**TG page 101**

# Adding detail

Sentence level

## Aims
■ to give further practice in using adjectives
■ to introduce regular plural nouns (those created by adding 's')

## Teaching notes
Most nouns change from singular to plural by adding 's'. This is the regular plural form used in thousands of nouns. There are only a few hundred nouns with irregular plural forms but these follow a number of predictable rules. The changing of 'y' to 'i', the use of 'es', and irregular plural forms are dealt with at a later level.

Unit 4

## Related activities

PCM 31
TG page 102

- PCM 31 (Plurals) offers further practice in identifying and using plural nouns.

- Give children a passage written in the singular and ask them to change it to the plural, or vice-versa.

- Ask groups of children to compile lists of plural nouns. Do any of the nouns have endings other than 's'?

PB page 53

# Describing a game

## Aims

Text and
word level

- to write a descriptive account
- to use alphabetical order (on the first letter only)

## Teaching notes

Children will find it useful to have access to a dictionary, alphabet chart or alphabet book to check their answers.

ANSWERS

2 Ahmed, Betty, Cheng, David, Gordon, Mitra, Rashida, Sally, Tanya, Winston, Yasmine, Zoe.

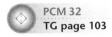
**PCM 32**
**TG page 103**

## Related activities

- PCM 32 (Alphabetical order) gives children further practice in ordering letters (two letters) alphabetically.

- Give children a selection of fiction books and get them to sort these into alphabetical order using the author surname.

PB pages 54–55

# Using charts

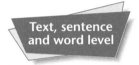
Text, sentence and word level

## Aims

- to interpret information given as a chart
- to introduce and use sequential knowledge of months of the year
- to give further practice in using adjectives

## Teaching notes

This activity demands very close reading. If you are introducing the activity to the class you may want to show them how to scan the chart and how to look for specific words. If children require support, concentrate on choosing the key word to be found. An encyclopaedia is useful for looking up details of patron saints.

---

**ANSWERS**

1. **a** St Valentine's Day is on February 14th.
   **b** Bastille Day
   **c** Any two of the following: Chinese New Year, Mother's Day, Eid-Ul-Fitr, Fête des Mères, Dragon Boat Festival, Notting Hill Carnival, Harvest Festival, Divali, Hanuka
   **d** Hanuka
2. **a** November.   **b** March   **c** July   **d** August
4. St George/England/April 23rd
   St Andrew/Scotland/November 30th
   St David/Wales/March 1st

---

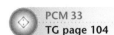
**PCM 33**
**TG page 104**

## Related activities

- PCM 33 (Months of the year) tests children's knowledge of the order and spelling of the months.

- Groups of children could undertake research into the stories connected to each patron saint.

PB page 56

# Exclamation marks

Word level

## Aims

- to introduce exclamations
- to give further practice using exclamation marks

## Teaching notes

Exclamations are one of the four sentence types. The others – statements, commands and questions – are studied at other points in the book. Exclamations express strong feeling and end in an exclamation mark. Some exclamations may be atypical (minor) sentences which have no verb.

### ANSWERS

1 Any of several, such as: **a** Oh no! **b** It's lovely! **c** Oh my goodness!
2 **a** Get Well card **b** birthday, a badge

## Related activity

- Look for examples of exclamations in cartoon strips.

PB page 57

# Commas in lists

Sentence level

## Aims

- to use commas to separate items in a list
- to begin to understand that commas separate nouns and phrases

## Teaching notes

Commas are used to improve clarity in writing. Although they are the commonest punctuation mark of all, they are used in a wide variety of ways. At this level only commas in lists are addressed. It is important that children realize that lists may be lists of nouns, but can also be lists of phrases.

## Related activity

PCM 34
TG page 105

- PCM 34 (Commas in lists) gives further practice in using commas.

PB pages 58–59

# Writing a report

Text level

## Aims

- to select a celebration and brainstorm ideas
- to note key points and details
- to draft a report
- to reconsider a previously written draft, amending where appropriate
- to rewrite the text appropriately

## Teaching notes

This activity draws together the skills used in Unit 4 so that the children can use them to write a report rather like the lead text at the start of the unit. This spread can be done in one long session or as a number of shorter sessions. Doing the activities as a number of shorter sessions offers you the chance to use both products (drafts, notes, etc.) and observation for assessment purposes.

If you wish to do a teacher introduction we suggest that you take the opportunity to do a shared rereading of the lead report and remind the class about the main structural features of a report - an introductory definition or classification, further information and a conclusion.

## ASSESSMENT POINTS

As you observe children working, you may wish to bear in mind to what extent children can do the following:

### Make notes

■ at this level children should begin to be able to brainstorm ideas about the special day
■ they may be able to add important details

### First draft

■ includes a definition of the subject of the report at the start
■ has sentences about various parts of the celebration

### Revise

■ reads text through to another child
■ discusses the passage with a partner

### Edit

■ locates his/her own spelling, grammar and punctuation mistakes

### Final draft

■ sets out text appropriately, with title, labels, capitals and punctuation in place

## Related activities

The assessment PCMs at the back of this book can also be used to assess some of these features.

cake
swimming **BIRTHDAY** gran
friends present

**Teacher's observations**

Most of the ideas from the notes have been used in completing the writing frame. The child has used the present consistently throughout and has got the right parts of the verb 'to be' throughout. Following revision, the sentences all make sense although in the first draft some full stops were missing. The child has added these in although he had to be prompted to look for them. The spelling is erratic but the child has located a good proportion of the spelling errors, with some prompting.

A special day

For my birthday I ~~have~~ had cake. It was a brown tran cake and it was choclate. ~~Their~~ There was lots left over. We had little sosages and twiglets.

We wear out best things on birthdays. I wore my tracksuit for tea at grans flat and bathers to go to the centre for swimming.

We do specill things like swimming and parties for birthday treats. Gary went to the roller skating but I was not old enough.

# UNIT 1 Writing to instruct

Name _____ Group _____ Date _____

| ASSESSMENT POINT *Can the child:* | PB page or PCM | Comments |
|---|---|---|
| **Text level** | | |
| *read* and understand a report | 46, 47 | |
| recognize the structural features of report (*definition, details, diagram* or *pictures*) | 46, 47 PCM 27 | |
| *plan* a report using rough notes | 58 | |
| read an invitation, recognizing detail | PCM 29 | |
| draft from detailed notes | 59 | |
| produce a final draft with appropriate punctuation and grammar | 59 | |
| answer literal and inferential comprehension questions | 40, 50, 55 PCM 28 | |
| design a celebration card | 49 | |
| design an invitation | 50 | |
| read from a calendar, extracting detail | 49 PCM 28 | |
| write a description, using adjectives | 51, 52, 53 PCM 30 | |
| **Sentence level** | | |
| complete sentences so that they make sense | 48 PCM 34 | |
| use *exclamations*, including *exclamation marks* | 56 | |
| recognize *verb* to be and use in sentences (with subect agreement) | 48 | |
| recognize and use *adjectives* in sentences | 51, 52 PCM 30 | |
| recognize and use *plural nouns,* with agreement | 52 PCM 31 | |
| recognize and use *commas* in lists within sentences | 57 PCM 34 | |
| **Word level** | | |
| know and use days of the week | 49 | |
| Know and use months of the year | 55 PCM 33 | |
| use alphabetical order (to first letter) (to second letter) | 53 PCM 32 | |
| Know and use singular and plural form nouns | 52 PCM 31 | |

# Celebration cards

Name _____ Date _____

**1** This report has got jumbled up. Cut out the sections and rearrange them so that the report is clear.

Birthday cards may have a number on the front showing how old the person getting the card is.

Celebration cards are cards we send to mark a special event or a special time of year.

Then the person who gets the card knows who it is from.

These cards usually have pictures on them and a special message inside.

**Celebration cards**

Some examples of celebration cards are birthday cards, congratulations cards and cards for religious events such as Christmas and Divali.

The sender of a card usually signs their name inside the card.

People send celebration cards to their family and friends to let them know they are thinking about them during the special event.

They usually say 'Happy Birthday' inside.

# Days of the week

Name _____ Date _____

July

Sports' day

| M | | 6 | 13 | 20 | 27 | — school trip |
| T | | 7 | 14 | 21 | 28 | |
| W | 1 | 8 | 15 | 22 | 29 | |
| T | 2 | 9 | 16 | 23 | 30 | |
| F | 3 | 10 | 17 | 24 | 31 | — last day of school |
| S | 4 | 11 | 18 | 25 | | |
| S | 5 | 12 | 19 | 26 | | |

Ann's birthday

August

Spain

| M | | 3 | 10 | 17 | 24 | 31 |
| T | | 4 | 11 | 18 | 25 | |
| W | | 5 | 12 | 19 | 26 | — Gran's |
| T | | 6 | 13 | 20 | 27 | — dentist |
| F | | 7 | 14 | 21 | 28 | |
| S | 1 | 8 | 15 | 22 | 29 | |
| S | 2 | 9 | 16 | 23 | 30 | |

On which day of the week do these events happen?

**a** Sports' day is on a _____ .

**b** Ann's birthday is on a _____ .

**c** The school trip is on a _____ .

**d** The first day of the school holidays is a _____ .

**e** There is an overnight visit to Gran on a _____ .

**f** The holiday in Spain begins on a _____ .

All the answers are a day of the week. Check your
spelling of these words.

# Rebus invitations

Name _____ Date _____

These invitations are a bit of a puzzle. Work them out and write them out using words instead of pictures.

D[ear] Sally,

Please come 2 m[y] fancy party. It starts at 3 o'[clock] [I] hope U [can] come.

love from Ben

Dear B[en]

U R invited to my [tea] ~~pot~~ party.

[at] :32 [castle] Road.

On: Friday 30th from [6] 2 [9]

love from Sally

© OUP: This page may be reproduced for class use solely within the purchaser's school or college

# *Describing toys*

Name _____ Date _____

This page from a toy catalogue is not yet finished. The descriptions of some toys have not been written.

This fluffy pink rabbit has long floppy ears and big blue eyes. In its paws it holds a juicy carrot.

**1** Write a description under each toy. Remember to use adjectives.

**2** Now colour in the pictures to match your description.

# *Plurals*

Name _____ Date _____

**1** Cut out the pictures and the labels. Match them together.

blower

balloon

sandwich

card

candle

present

jelly

cake

**2** All of the labels are singular. Change them into plural labels if the picture shows more than one of anything.

# Alphabetical order

Name _____ Date _____

These are the children from Rashida's class. Fill in the class register using the children's names to sort them into order. Sometimes you will have to look at the second letter of their name.

Yasmine

Cheng

Ahmed

Daisy

Blossom

Eric

Paul

Zak

Tanya

Douglas

Mustafa

Claire

Sally

Simon

Quentin

Alex

Winston

Satwinder

Zoe

Michael

**Class Register**

# Months of the year

Name _____  Date _____

In this poem the names of the months have been
missed out. Put in the missing words. Check you have
spelt them correctly. Then copy out the poem in your
best handwriting.

January snowy

_____ flowy

_____ blowy

_____ showery

_____ flowery

_____ bowery

July moppy

_____ croppy

_____ poppy

_____ breezy

_____ wheeezy

December freezy

# Commas in lists

Name _____ Date _____

**1** Complete these lists.

| 4 things I can see in the classroom | 4 things I can see through the window | 4 things I eat at lunch-time |
|---|---|---|
| | | |

| 4 things I play at playtime | 4 people I like | 4 T.V. programmes I watch |
|---|---|---|
| | | |

**2** Use your lists to finish these sentences. Think about where the commas go.

**a** In my classroom I can see a _____ _____ _____

and _____ .

**b** I can see _____ _____ _____ and _____

through the window.

**c** For lunch I eat _____ _____ _____ and _____ .

**d** I play _____ _____ and _____ at playtime.

**e** _____ _____ and _____ are all people I like.

**f** I watch _____ _____ _____

and _____ .

# General photocopy masters

**PCM**

( **Introduction** )

| | |
|---|---|
| **PCM 35** | ***Two column X 6 row grid***<br>This table can be photocopied and used for a range of activities. |
| **PCM 36** | ***Three column X 6 row grid***<br>This table can be photocopied and used for a range of activities.<br>It may be particularly useful for the activities on page5 but can be used for many other activities. |
| **PCM 37** | ***Flow chart for sequencing events***<br>This graphic organizer is useful for helping children to plan story sequence.<br>It can be photocopied and used for a range of activities. It may be particularly useful for the activities on pages 27 and 30 in Unit 2 but can be used for many other activities. |
| **PCM 38** | ***Drafting code***<br>These are the marks used for editing and revisions in these books.<br>You may want to use these same marks in demonstrating editing and revision on a large text. If you would like the children to use these marks, this PCM can be copied as a poster or reminder card. This system of marks is only intended as a guide and it will naturally be most useful for you to customize it to the system in your class. Most schools have a marking policy and you may wish to include editing marks in this. |
| **PCM 39** | ***Play the dictionary game***<br>This PCM offers practice in using a dictionary. It is not linked to a particular unit and can be used at any time. |
| **PCM 40** | ***Sentences***<br>This PCM gives children the chance to practise capital letters and full stops.<br>It is not linked to a particular unit and can be used at any time. |
| **PCM 41** | ***Revising sentences***<br>This PCM gives the children the chance to consolidate their understanding about sentences. |

Name _____. Date _____

Name _____ Date _____

# Flow chart for sequencing events

Name _____ Date _____

Beginning

Middle

Ending

# *Drafting code*

Name _____ Date _____

## REVISING YOUR WRITING

Read through and consider these questions.

**1** Does it make sense?

**2** Is it a good length?

**3** Does it start and end well?

**4** Is anything missing?

> Things you might mark:
>
> something is hard to understand: ～～～
>
> something is left out: ⋏

## EDITING YOUR WRITING

Read through and consider these questions.

**1** Is it written in sentences?

**2** Do the sentences sound right when you read them out?

**3** Check the use of:

- capital letters
- full stops
- question marks
- commas
- speech marks

**4** If any are in the wrong place or missing, mark them.

> Things you might mark:
>
> a full stop: ⊙
>
> a capital letter: c̲
>
> words in the wrong order: ∽
>
> spelling mistakes: SP

# Play the Dictionary Game

Name _____     Date _____

**1** You will need a dictionary and a pencil.

Look in your dictionary and see which is the first word that begins with f.

Write it here: _____

Now find the last word beginning with f.

Write it here: _____

**2** Now play with a partner and see who is the quickest at finding the first and last words that begin with these letters

| | first word | last word |
|---|---|---|
| y | | |
| m | | |
| b | | |
| t | | |
| w | | |
| g | | |
| k | | |
| p | | |

**3** Compare your answers and see if you agree.

# The Seal King's Daughter

Name _____   Date _____

Read this retelling of a traditional Scottish folk tale.

A long, long time ago a fisherman named Roderic lived in a remote part of Scotland. He was walking by the sea when he heard singing. Cautiously, he peered over the rocks. He saw three girls singing joyfully and playing in the surf. Roderic did not look long, for he knew at once that he had seen the seal king's daughters, who could turn into seals. As he was leaving he saw some beautiful seal skins shining in the sun. So he took one home with him and hid it under the roof.

Later that evening, as Roderic mended his nets, he heard a knock at the door. Outside stood the fairest woman he had ever seen. 'Please help me. I have lost my silken seal skin and cannot return to the sea until I find it again,' she said. Roderic thought how pleasant his life would be with her as his wife, so he said that he did not know where her seal skin was. Instead, he asked her to be his wife. The seal king's daughter lifted her sorrowful eyes to Roderic and said, 'If I cannot find my seal skin and go back to the sea I have no choice but to be your wife, for you have been kind to me.' So Roderic and his seal wife were married and had three children: Donald, Thomas and little Katie.

One day, little Katie asked her mother, 'Why does father keep a seal skin under the roof?' The seal wife knew at once that it was her skin. She took her children down to the sea and said, 'I will always love you, but now I have to go back to the sea. Listen to the sound of the sea on windy days and you will hear me.' With that she grabbed her seal skin and disappeared into the sea.

Roderic and his children missed their mother very much, but when they went fishing they always caught ten times as many fish as anyone else. And when the wind blew from the sea they seemed to hear her singing.

**1** Underline the two main characters in the story in red.

**2** Underline the place where the story happens in blue.

**3** Underline the words which tell you when the story happened in green.

**4** Underline the names of the children in yellow.

# Comprehension

Name _____  Date _____

**1** Find these words in the text from The Seal King's Daughter and try to work out what they mean, or look them up in the dictionary. Circle the correct answers.

**a cautiously** means

quickly        jumping        taking care

**b remote** means

a long way away        near        cold

**c joyfully** means

happily        sadly        slowly

**d grabbed** means

pushed        took quickly        hid

**2** Answer these questions.

**a** What did the seal king's daughter use her seal skin for?

**b** Where did Roderic hide the seal skin?

**c** What sort of person do you think Roderic was?

# Sequencing a story

Name _____ Date _____

**1** Here are four pictures from the story 'The Seal King's Daughter'.

Write a sentence to say what is happening in each picture.

1 ........................................................................................................

........................................................................................................

2 ........................................................................................................

........................................................................................................

3 ........................................................................................................

........................................................................................................

4 ........................................................................................................

........................................................................................................

# Fiction and non-fiction

Name _____    Date _____

Here is part of a page about seals.

Seals are mammals who have four flippers which they use to walk and swim. This makes them slow and clumsy on land. Once they have slipped into the water they can swim, twist and turn with ease.

Most seals hunt fish. They can hunt even in dark or murky water because the huge whiskers around their face can detect changes in water pressure.

Seals can remain in even very cold water for long periods. Beneath their skin they have a thick coat of special fat called blubber which keeps them warm. When they dive, seals can close their nostrils and ears. Some species can stay below the surface for 30 minutes.

**1** Add these labels to the diagram: nostrils, whiskers, ears, front flippers, rear flippers.

**2** Is this passage fiction or non-fiction?

**3** How can you tell whether this is a fiction or non-fiction text?

**4** Underline the sentence in the passage which says what seals eat.

**5** Underline the word in the passage which means seal fat.

**6** What do you think the weather is like where seals live?

# *Grammar activity: sentences.*

Name _____  Date _____

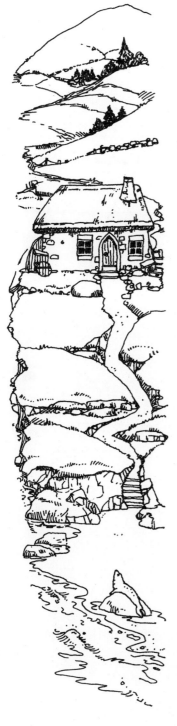

**1** Rearrange these words to make sentences, adding capital letters and punctuation.

   **a** swim seals can fast very

   **b** hid seal skin the Roderic

   **c** was the seal king's beautiful daughter


**2** Add full stops or question marks to the sentences below.

   **a** Where is my seal skin

   **b** Roderic lived by the sea

   **c** Seals have fat under their skins

   **d** What do seals eat


**3** Underline the verbs in these sentences. The first one is done for you.

   **a** The seal <u>slipped</u> into the sea.

   **b** Roderic looked around the rocks.

   **c** The seal wife ran along the beach.

   **d** The seals chased the fish.


**4** Put verbs into these sentences so that they make sense.

   **a** Roderic _____ a beautiful woman.

   **b** The children _____ for their mother.

   **c** The seals _____ on the beach.

   **d** Seals _____ in cold water.

# Punctuation: writing speech

Name _____  Date _____

**1** Read this dialogue.

'Where is my seal skin?' asked the seal wife.
'I don't know,' said Roderic.

**2** Write what the character said into the speech bubbles.

**3** Write out what the seal and fish say.

'_____,' yelled the seal.

'_____,' cried the fish.

**4** Complete the sentences to show who is speaking.

'We are safe! ' _____ .

'Where have they gone, ' _____ .

# Riddles and rhyme

Name ............................................................... Date ...............

1 Read these riddles and discuss what they are about (the answers are at the foot of the page).

**a** I fly like a bird,
And buzz like a bee.
Got a tail like a fish,
Got a hop like a flea.
What am I ?

**b** A skin have I
More eyes than one
I can be nice when
I am done.
What am I?

2 In each riddle, underline two words which rhyme with each other.

3 Choose words to rhyme with the following

skin rhymes with ........................... .

tail rhymes with ........................... .

4 Write words which mean the same as the words below.

EXAMPLE: very big — huge

**a** very small ...........................

**b** noisy ...........................

**c** sad ...........................

5 Sort these words into alphabetical order.

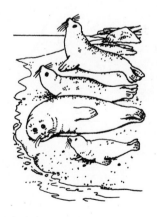

seal
mother
potato
beach
helicopter

(a) a helicopter   (b) a potato

# Planning a postcard

Name _____  Date _____

Look at this cartoon.

**1** Imagine you are the child who saw this happen. You are going to write a postcard to a friend to tell them what happened.

Choose an address for your friend. You need a house or flat number, a road, a town and a county

**2** Now make a timeline of the events you want to tell your friend.

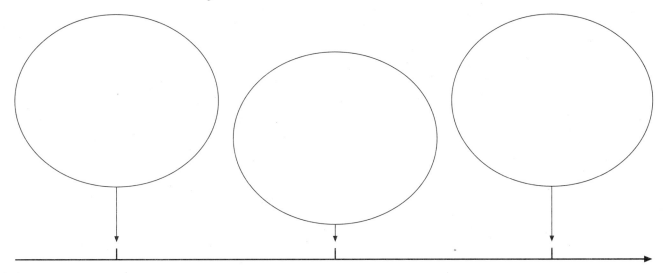

**3** Write a description of the seal and a description of the seagull. Make sure you use two adjectives to describe each character.

The seal was _____ .

The seagull was _____ .

# *Writing a postcard*

Name _____ Date _____

1 Now write a draft of your postcard. Make sure you have:

- an address
- a greeting
- the events in order, with lots of detail to make it interesting
- a closure

2 Choose one of these closures for your postcard:

a Love from,

b Yours sincerely,

c Best wishes,

Dear _____

# PCMs ASSESSMENT UNIT

Name _____  Group _____  Date _____

| ASSESSMENT POINT *The child:* | PCM | | | | |
|---|---|---|---|---|---|
| **Text level** | | | | | |
| read and understand narrative opening of a traditional tale | 40 | | | | |
| read rhyming riddles with intonation and humor | 46 | | | | |
| read and select information for non-fiction text | 43 | | | | |
| infer *meaning* of words from text or looks up | 41 | | | | |
| select *characters* from text | 40 | | | | |
| select temporal and locational *setting* from text | 40 | | | | |
| answer literal, inferential and evaluative questions | 41 | | | | |
| discriminate between fiction and non-fiction, and give reasons | 43 | | | | |
| sequence events in order | 42, 47 | | | | |
| plan address | 47–48 | | | | |
| plan opening sentence and events in order | 48 | | | | |
| select appropriate closure | 48 | | | | |
| draft postcard | 48 | | | | |
| **Sentence level** | | | | | |
| label a diagram using *nouns* | 43 | | | | |
| write a description using *adjectives* | 47 | | | | |
| arrange appropriate word order | 44 | | | | |
| recognize that *sentences* make sense | 44 | | | | |
| insert *verbs* in a sentence | 44 | | | | |
| use *capital letters* in sentences (start and proper nouns) | 44 | | | | |
| use *question marks* in sentence | 44 | | | | |
| identify *direct speech* | 45 | | | | |
| write direct direct speech in *speech bubbles* | 45 | | | | |
| **Word level** | | | | | |
| choose *rhyming words* | 46 | | | | |
| identify *rhyme* in riddles | 46 | | | | |
| identify synomyns | 46 | | | | |
| sort words by first letter of *alphabetical order* | 46 | | | | |
| Look up words in a dictionary | 41 | | | | |

*General PCMs*

# Glossary

adjective | A word that describes a noun. It may come before or after the noun. Categories of adjective include:

**Number** EXAMPLE: five, twenty, a million
**Quantity** EXAMPLE: more, some, half
**Quality** EXAMPLE: blue, big, fishy
**Possessive** EXAMPLE: his, my, your
**Interrogative** EXAMPLE: which, what, whose

There are degrees of adjectives.

**Nominative** (the quality) EXAMPLE: big
**Comparative** (the degree of the quality) EXAMPLE: bigger
**Superlative** (the limit of the quality) EXAMPLE: biggest

Some adjectives can be made into adverbs by the addition of -ly.
EXAMPLE: Serious - seriously

account | A piece of speech or writing which tells us about an event.

adverb | An adverb is a word or phrase which describes or modifies a verb. Many adverbs have the suffix -ly. Adverbs can be considered in a number of categories:

**Adverbs of time** (temporal) EXAMPLE: later, now, soon
**Adverbs of manner** EXAMPLE: firmly, happily
**Adverbs of place** EXAMPLE: here, there, far

Some adverbs have little to do with verbs. Adverbs of degree add extra meaning to the next word. EXAMPLES: very, rather, really. Some adverbs join sentences together. EXAMPLES: however, moreover, nevertheless.

alliteration | A phrase where adjacent or closely connected words begin with the same phoneme (sound). EXAMPLES: ten tired teddies, sliding slithery snakes

antonym | A word with the opposite meaning to another word. EXAMPLES: hot-cold, old-new

apostrophe | A punctuation mark used to show contraction.
**Auxiliary verbs** (to be and to have) EXAMPLES: it's, I've, we've, they're
**Negatives** EXAMPLES: didn't, won't
**Figures** EXAMPLES: '60s, '90s
Apostrophes also indicate possession. Before the 's' for most single nouns. EXAMPLE: girl's dress. After the 's' for most plural nouns. EXAMPLE: girls' dresses. (But note children's) Possessive 'its' does not have an apostrophe.

blurb | A piece of writing that gives a short account of the content of a book. It is usually found on the outside cover or inside the cover.

brainstorm | A way of writing down ideas when planning writing. Words are arranged around the topic you are thinking about.

bullet point | A mark like a fat full stop which is used to emphasize items in a list.

category word | A word which describes a set of items. EXAMPLE: the category word 'footwear' includes shoes, slippers, socks, etc.

capital letter | The capital letters are: ABCDEFGHIJKLMNOPQRSTUVWXYZ.
The capital letters may be referred to as 'upper case' letters and the small letters as 'lower case' letters.

| | |
|---|---|
| character | A person, animal or other being who takes part in a story. |
| chronological order | The order in which events happen. Chronological writing includes the events in a time ordered sequence. EXAMPLE: an account of a day, starting in the morning and going through to the evening. |
| closure | The word or phrase used before the writer's signature at the end of a letter. EXAMPLES: Yours sincerely, yours faithfully, love from, yours truly |
| comma | A mark used to break up sentences so that they are easier to understand. Commas are used to separate items in a list which is part of a sentence. EXAMPLE: I bought eggs, fish, peas and some chocolate. |
| compound word | A word made from two other words. EXAMPLES: footpath, doghouse |
| common gender word | A word which can refer to men, women or both. EXAMPLES: passenger, doctor |
| connective | A connective is a word or phrase used to link clauses or sentences together. Various types of words or phrases can work as connectives:<br>**Conjunctions** EXAMPLES: and, but, because<br>**Adverbs** EXAMPLE: finally<br>**Prepositional expressions** EXAMPLE: in other words<br>Connectives are important in maintaining the cohesion of a text in a number of ways:<br>**Addition** EXAMPLES: and, also<br>**Apposition** EXAMPLES: however, but<br>**Cause** EXAMPLES: because, this means that<br>**Time** EXAMPLES: next, just then |
| conjunction | A conjunction is a word used to join parts of a sentence. EXAMPLES: and, but, because<br>Temporal conjunctions tell us about time. EXAMPLES: then, next, after |
| consonant/vowel | In the English alphabet there are 5 vowels (aeiou) and 21 consonants (bcdfghjklmnpqrstvwxyz).<br>In English speech there are 20 vowel sounds and 24 consonant sounds, depending on accent. |
| definition | A statement of the meaning of a word. There is a definition for each word in a dictionary entry. |
| dictionary entry | Information given about a word in a dictionary, usually including the meaning, word class, related forms of a word and an EXAMPLE or EXAMPLES of use. |
| draft | A preliminary written form of a piece of writing.<br>Also the process of working on the composition of a document. |
| edit | To change written work, especially grammar, spelling, punctuation and vocabulary, in preparation for publishing. |
| exclamation | A type of sentence expressing emotion that is concluded with an exclamation mark. Exclamations can be short sentences without verbs. EXAMPLE: Help! |
| exclamation mark | A punctuation mark used at the end of a sentence to indicate strong emotion. |
| fiction/non-fiction | Fiction is an invented story, poem or play. Non-fiction is writing about real events, feelings or things. |
| first person pronoun | The first person pronoun is 'I'. Pronouns (words which can be used in place of nouns) can be set out with verbs as on page 164. |

|      | **Singular** | **Plural** |
|------|--------------|------------|
| 1st  | I am         | we are     |
| 2nd  | you are      | you are    |
| 3rd  | he/she/it is | they are   |

**formal language/ informal language**    Formal language is the speech and writing we use in formal situations. Informal language is used in informal situations. The formality of language is determined by the grammar and vocabulary used.

**gender words (masculine and feminine)**    Words that indicate gender, usually nouns. EXAMPLES: prince, princess

**genre**    A genre is a type of writing (or speech) that achieves a particular social purpose. In doing so, certain structural and language features become characteristic of particular genres. For instance, a recount tells the reader what has happened and in doing so usually uses the first person, the past tense and chronologically ordered writing.

Genres rarely exist in totally pure forms or in isolation.

Common genres include: Fiction − mysteries, plays, poetry, romance, science fiction, etc; Non-fiction − recount, discussion, explanation, report, persuasion, instruction

**greeting**    The words used to begin a letter. Usually Dear... The use of given or family names in the greeting depends on the level of formality of the letter.

**homonyms**    Words with the same form but different meanings.

**introduction**    The beginning of a piece of writing.

**imperative**    An imperative word or sentence commands or tells the reader or listener to do something. EXAMPLE: Shut the door.

**language**    Language is what people use to share their thoughts with each other. We talk with our voices. This is spoken language. When we write we make written language.

**noun**    A word that names a thing or feeling. Nouns can be singular (one) or plural (more than one).
**Proper nouns**: name particular things or feelings. Proper nouns start with capital letters. EXAMPLE: Fred
**Common nouns**: name a sort of thing. EXAMPLE: man
**Collective noun**: names a group of people or things. EXAMPLE: flock
**Abstract noun**: names a concept, idea or feeling. EXAMPLE: love.

**onomatopoeia**    Words which echo sounds associated with their meaning. EXAMPLES: clang, hiss

**persuade**    To persuade is to try to make or convince someone to do something.

**plan**    The intentions of the writer for a piece of writing before a draft is written. Plans can be in the form of thoughts, notes and pictures.

**plot**    The narrative element in fiction and drama. The plot is distinguished from the story by the causal quality which links episodes, reveals significances and reaches a conclusion.

**plural**    More than one. For regular nouns the plural is formed by adding an inflectional suffix (-s). Many nouns are irregular. EXAMPLES: feet, children

**poem**    A text which uses features such as rhythm, rhyme, syntax or vocabulary to convey ideas.

| | |
|---|---|
| **preposition** | A word describing the relationship between two nouns (or pronouns or a noun and a pronoun). EXAMPLES: on, under, in. Traditionally it has been considered incorrect to finish a sentence with a preposition but this can lead to awkward sentences and is no longer considered incorrect. |
| **proper noun** | See noun. |
| **punctuation** | A way of marking written text to help understanding. |
| **question** | A type of sentence which demands a response from the reader or listener. A question ends in a question mark. |
| **question mark** | The punctuation mark that goes at the end of a question. |
| **recount** | A recount is a (usually non-fiction) text type which informs the reader about events which have happened. Recount is characterized by chronological order, particular participants and the use of the past tense. Recounts may take the form of narratives, letters, books, etc. |
| **revise** | To examine and amend a written piece. Usually refers to making qualitative changes, rather than spelling or other transcription details. |
| **rhyme** | Words containing the same sound in their final syllable are said to rhyme. EXAMPLES: man, pan |
| **rhythm** | The pattern of stressed syllables when writing is read aloud or spoken. |
| **sentence** | A sentence is a piece of language that can stand by itself and make sense. In writing, the first word of a sentence starts with a capital letter and the sentence ends with a full stop(.), exclamation mark (!), or question mark(?). |
| **setting** | The place and time of events in a story. |
| **simile** | A sentence or phrase which creates an image in the reader's mind by comparing the subject to something else. EXAMPLE: As free as a bird |
| **singular** | The form of the noun which indicates one of something. |
| **slogan** | A slogan is a sentence that aims to make us remember something or grab our attention. EXAMPLES: Slip, slap, slop (slip on a shirt, slap on a hat, slop on the suncream) |
| **speech marks** | Inverted commas which indicate which words are actually spoken in direct speech. Speech marks enclose any punctuation which belongs to the sentence spoken. A comma is enclosed within the speech marks when an utterance is interrupted. EXAMPLE: "But he can't," she said, "he can't do it!" |
| **statement** | A sentence which gives information but does not demand a response. |
| **tense, past tense, present tense** | Tense tells us when something is happening. **Past**: something has already happened. (Simple past: I talked to my friend yesterday. Past perfect refers to an event with current relevance: I've broken the window.) **Present**: something is happening now. (Simple present: He goes past every day. Progressive present: He is reading a timetable.) **Future**: something will or may happen. There is no tense choice for the imperative: Play more quietly; or the subjunctive: We insisted that he play more quietly. |
| **title** | The heading of a piece of writing. |
| **verb** | A verb is a word that tells us what people are doing or being. |
| **verse** | A part of a poem with a particular theme. It may have a characteristic rhyme scheme and rhythm. |
| **vocabulary** | Our vocabulary is the words we know and use. |

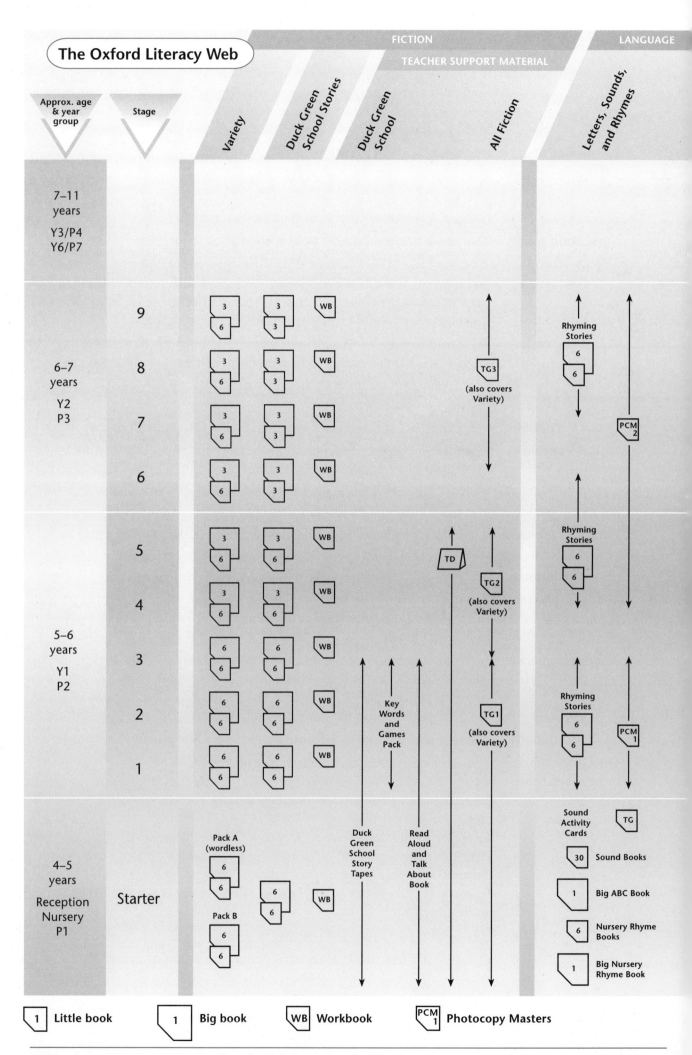

# The Oxford Literacy Web

FICTION — LANGUAGE

TEACHER SUPPORT MATERIAL

| Approx. age & year group | Stage | Variety | Duck Green School Stories | Duck Green School | All Fiction | Letters, Sounds, and Rhymes |
|---|---|---|---|---|---|---|
| 7–11 years Y3/P4 Y6/P7 | | | | | | |
| 6–7 years Y2 P3 | 9 | 3 6 | 3 3 | WB | | Rhyming Stories 6 6 |
| | 8 | 3 6 | 3 3 | WB | TG3 (also covers Variety) | |
| | 7 | 3 6 | 3 3 | WB | | PCM 2 |
| | 6 | 3 6 | 3 3 | WB | | |
| 5–6 years Y1 P2 | 5 | 3 6 | 3 6 | WB | TD | Rhyming Stories 6 6 |
| | 4 | 3 6 | 3 6 | WB | TG2 (also covers Variety) | |
| | 3 | 6 6 | 6 6 | WB | Key Words and Games Pack | Rhyming Stories |
| | 2 | 6 6 | 6 6 | WB | TG1 (also covers Variety) | 6 6 PCM 1 |
| | 1 | 6 6 | 6 6 | WB | | |
| 4–5 years Reception Nursery P1 | Starter | Pack A (wordless) 6 6 Pack B 6 6 | 6 6 | WB | Duck Green School Story Tapes · Read Aloud and Talk About Book | Sound Activity Cards · TG 30 Sound Books · 1 Big ABC Book · 6 Nursery Rhyme Books · 1 Big Nursery Rhyme Book |

| 1 | Little book | 1 | Big book | WB | Workbook | PCM 1 | Photocopy Masters |
|---|---|---|---|---|---|---|---|

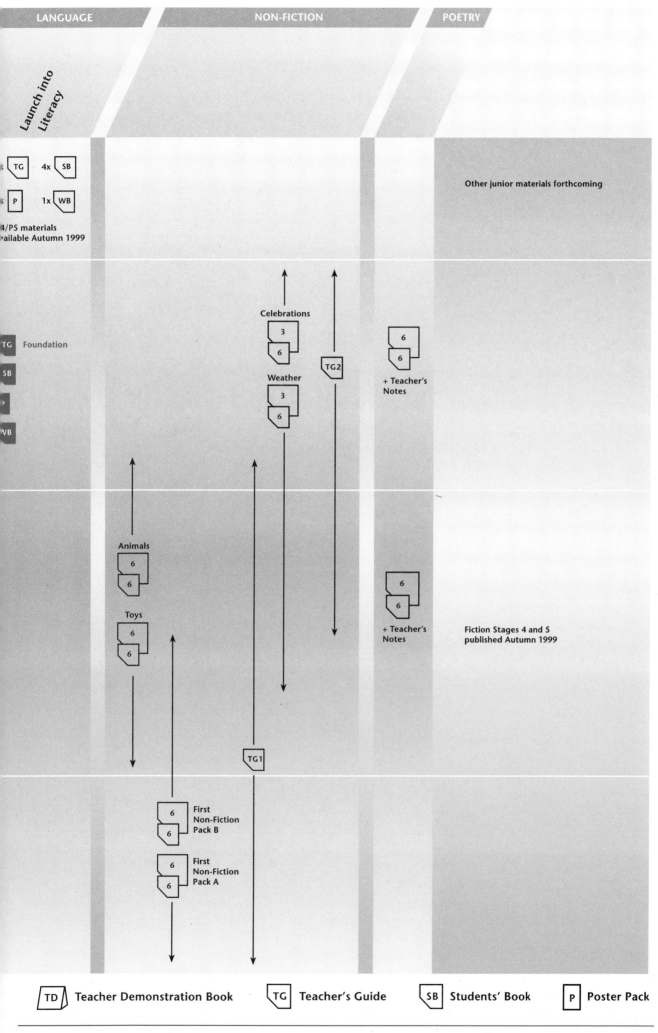

Launch into Literacy

TG    4x SB

P    1x WB

4/P5 materials
ailable Autumn 1999

Other junior materials forthcoming

TG   Foundation

SB

VB

Celebrations

3

6

Weather

3

6

TG2

6

6

+ Teacher's
Notes

Animals

6

6

Toys

6

6

6

6

+ Teacher's
Notes

Fiction Stages 4 and 5
published Autumn 1999

TG1

6   First
Non-Fiction
6   Pack B

6   First
Non-Fiction
6   Pack A

TD  Teacher Demonstration Book     TG  Teacher's Guide     SB  Students' Book     P  Poster Pack